DENYS THE AREOPAGITE

OUTSTANDING CHRISTIAN THINKERS

Series Editor: Brian Davies OP, Professor of Philosophy at Fordham University, New York.

Cappadocians
Anthony Meredith SJ

Hans Urs von Balthasar
John O'Donnell SJ

Augustine
Mary T. Clark RSCJ

Teresa of Avila
Archbishop Rowan Williams

Catherine of Siena
Giuliana Cavallini OP

Bultmann
David Fergusson

Kierkegaard
Julia Watkin

Karl Barth
John Webster

Lonergan
Frederick Rowe SJ

Aquinas
Brian Davies OP

Reinhold Neibuhr
Kenneth Durkin

Paul Tillich
John Heywood Thomas

Venerable Bede
Benedicta Ward SLG

Karl Rahner
William V. Dych SJ

Apostolic Fathers
Simon Tugwell OP

Anselm
G. R. Evans

Denys the Areopagite
Andrew Louth

DENYS THE AREOPAGITE

Andrew Louth

continuum
LONDON • NEW YORK

Continuum

The Tower Building, 11 York Road, London SE1 7NX
370 Lexington Avenue, New York, NY, 10017-6503

www.continuumbooks.com

First published 1989

Re-issued 2001

British library Cataloguing-in-Publication Data
A catalogue record for this book is available from The British Library

ISBN 0 8264 5772 X

Contents

Editorial Foreword

St Anselm of Canterbury (1033–1109) once described himself as someone with faith seeking understanding. In words addressed to God he says 'I long to understand in some degree thy truth, which my heart believes and loves. For I do not seek to understand that I may believe, but believe in order to understand.'

This is what Christians have always inevitably said, either explicitly or implicitly. Christianity rests on faith, but it also has content. It teaches and proclaims a distinctive and challenging view of reality. It naturally encourages reflection. It is something to think about; something about which one might even have second thoughts.

But what have the greatest Christian thinkers said? And is it worth saying? Does it engage with modern problems? Does it provide us with a vision to live by? Does it make sense? Can it be preached? Is it believable?

The Outstanding Christian Thinkers series is offered to readers with questions like these in mind. It aims to provide clear, authoritative and critical accounts of outstanding Christian writers from New Testament times to the present. It ranges across the full spectrum of Christian thought to include Catholic and Protestant thinkers, thinkers from East and West, thinkers ancient, mediaeval and modern.

The series draws on the best scholarship currently available, so it will interest all with a professional concern for the history of Christian ideas. But contributors also write for general readers who have little or no previous knowledge of the subjects to be dealt with. Its volumes should therefore prove helpful at a popular as well as an academic level. For the most part they are devoted to a single thinker, but occasionally the subject is a movement or school of thought.

Brian Davies OP

Bibliography

DENYS'S WORKS

The works of Denys the Areopagite are printed in: *Patrologia Graeca* 3, ed. J.-P. Migne (Paris, 1857), from the edition by Baltha-sar Corderius (2 vols, Antwerp, 1634). A new critical edition is still awaited from Göttingen.

The translation in the *Classics of Western Spirituality* series, by Colm Luibheid and Paul Rorem (London/Mahwah, NJ, 1987) takes account of the Göttingen edition.

In this book, column references to Migne are frequently added (or used alone): these are printed in the margin of the Luibheid–Rorem translation.

English translations are usually my own, though sometimes I have used the Luibheid–Rorem translation. Even when I have not used their translation, I have found it most helpful.

OTHER BOOKS FREQUENTLY CITED

See p. x for the abbreviated forms of references used.

Pseudo-Dionysius, The Complete Works, trans. Colm Luibheid and Paul Rorem (*Classics of Western Spirituality*; London: SPCK/Mahwah, NJ: Paulist Press, 1987).

H. Koch, *Pseudo-Dionysius Areopagita in seinen Beziehungen zum Neoplatonismus und Mysterienwesen* (Mainz, 1900).

BIBLIOGRAPHY

J.-P. Migne (ed.), *Patrologia Graeca* (Paris, 1857–66).

R. Roques, *L'Univers dionysien. Structure hiérarchique du monde selon le Pseudo-Denys* (Paris, 1954).

R. Roques, *Structures théologiques de la gnose à Richard de Saint-Victor* (Paris, 1962).

Paul Rorem, *Biblical and Liturgical Symbols within the Pseudo-Dionysian Synthesis* (Toronto, 1984).

For further bibliography, see Roques, *L'Univers dionysien* . . . pp. 7–28, and Rorem, *Biblical and Liturgical Symbols* . . . pp. 151–6.

Abbreviations

CA   *Corpus Areopagiticum*
CH   *Celestial Hierarchy*
DN   *Divine Names*
EH   *Ecclesiastical Hierarchy*
Ep.   *Epistle*
MT   *Mystical Theology*
PG   J.-P. Migne (ed.), *Patrologia Graeca*

Works =
Pseudo-Dionysius, The Complete Works, trans. Colm Luibheid and Paul Rorem

Koch, *Ps-Dionysius* =
H. Koch, *Pseudo-Dionysius Areopagita in seinen Beziehungen zum Neoplatonismus und Mysterienwesen*

Roques, *L'Univers* =
R. Roques, *L'Univers dionysien. Structure hiérarchique du monde selon le Pseudo-Denys*

Roques, *Structures* =
R. Roques, *Structures théologiques de la gnose à Richard de Saint-Victor*

Rorem, *Symbols* =
Paul Rorem, *Biblical and Liturgical Symbols within the Pseudo-Dionysian Synthesis*

1

Introduction: the intellectual world of the late fifth century

A HIDDEN AUTHOR

At the beginning of the sixth century the Christian community began to become aware of a collection of writings, the *Corpus Areopagiticum* or the Areopagitical Corpus, that has exercised a profound influence on Christian theology from that day to this. For centuries it was thought that they were the works of that Dionysius (or Denys, as he became known in the vernacular) who is mentioned as having been converted by St Paul's defence before the Areopagus in Athens (Acts 17:34). The writings themselves locate their writer in first-century Christianity: he speaks of Paul as his mentor, addresses letters to Timothy and Titus, and even to the apostle John in exile on Patmos; he tells of experiencing the darkness that covered the earth at the time of the crucifixion (when he was in Egypt, still a pagan), and (perhaps) presents himself as present, with some of the apostles, at the death of the Blessed Virgin. Eusebius in his *Church History* (III.4.6) states that Denys the Areopagite became the first Bishop of Athens, basing this information on the testimony of another Denys, who was Bishop of Corinth at the end of the second century. Later tradition, in the West and especially in France, made Denys the Areopagite not only Bishop of Athens, but also the apostle to the Gauls and first Bishop of Paris who was martyred for the Christian faith on what is now Montmartre.

Gradually, however, this whole tradition was dismantled. Peter Abelard added to his troubles by questioning the theory that the martyr-bishop of Paris (and patron of the Abbey of Saint-Denis)

1

was the author of the *Corpus Areopagiticum*. Scholars from the time of the Renaissance onwards revived ancient doubts about the authenticity of these writings, and more recent research[1] has proved beyond any reasonable doubt that, far from being works from the first century, these writings belong to the end of the fifth or the beginning of the sixth century.[2] Denys the Areopagite became the Pseudo-Denys or Pseudo-Dionysius, and interest in him declined, apart from attempts to solve the fascinating problem as to who exactly he was. But interest in Denys could not lapse for long, for, whoever he was, his writings exercised an enormous influence on the so-called mystical tradition of the mediaeval West. As interest in that tradition increases as the twentieth century wears on, so curiosity, at least, about Denys and his writings has grown.

Denys veiled himself in the folds of a lightly-worn pseudonymity. The curiosity of modern scholarship has stripped off from him the veil he chose to wear, but has hardly come much closer to discovering his own true identity. Almost everyone in the period has been suggested, but few of the suggestions have convinced anyone other than their authors and none has gained general acceptance.[3] Even what virtually everyone accepts—that the author of the *Corpus Areopagiticum* belongs to the end of the fifth or beginning of the sixth century—reveals very little: it simply locates him in a period of the Church's history, little known and much misunderstood. So, as we cannot begin this study with an account of our author's life, perhaps we may begin with a sketch of the period of church history in the shadows of which he still hides himself. But it is indeed an obscure period—the ideal hiding-place for one such as our author—and in our attempt to make something clear of it some of the way will seem rather hard going. But, though obscure, it was a crucially important period in the life of the Church, and it is essential to come to terms with it, if we are ever to understand Denys.

CONFLICT OVER THE PERSON OF CHRIST

For most students of theology, the Council of Chalcedon, held in AD 451, represents the end of 'early Christian doctrine': after the council a darkness descends which only begins to clear in the Middle Ages, or at the Reformation, or sometimes even later still. The Council of Chalcedon is seen as settling the great Christological controversy of the patristic period which had begun almost two centuries earlier with the condemnation of Paul of Samosata at Antioch (268) and then the condemnation of Arius at Nicaea (325)—both for having questioned in different ways the full divinity of Christ—and continued through the heresy of Apollinaris (*c.* 310–*c.* 390), who compromised Christ's full humanity by denying him a human soul and was condemned at Constantinople (381), to culminate in the great Christological controversy between Alexandria and Antioch. This final stage of the controversy was concerned with the question of reconciling full divinity and full humanity in Christ.

The Alexandrian tradition, which can be traced back to Athanasius (Patriarch 328–373) and found its fullest expression in Cyril (Patriarch 412–446), started from the confession of the full divinity of the Word of God who, in the incarnation, united himself completely with humanity, so that the Incarnate Word of God was truly God among us, his mother was truly called *Theotokos* (God-bearer, or Mother of God), and by such divine contact with the human condition, the wretched, fallen state of mankind was healed. This emphasis on uncompromised divinity and unqualified unity was summed up in the phrase, dear to Cyril, 'one incarnate nature of God the Word'.

The opposing Antiochene tradition can be traced back to Diodore, Bishop of Tarsus (d. *c.* 390), if not to Eustathius, Bishop of Antioch (Bishop from *c.* 324 to 326), and found its most developed form in Theodore (*c.* 350–428), Bishop of Mopsuestia; though when the storm broke in 428, Theodore was dead and his disciple Nestorius (d. *c.* 451), the newly elected Bishop (or Patriarch) of Constantinople, bore the brunt of the conflict. For the Antiochenes, what was important was to hold firmly to both the full divinity and the full humanity of Christ. Christ's work of redemption was something worked out in *our* humanity: the sacrifice Christ offered he offered as man, and our redemption depends on his priestly role, which is something he exercises in *his* humanity. Certainly Christ is fully divine, too: God takes the initiative in our redemption and the human, priestly work of Christ is in response to that divine initiative. Christ is seen as so utterly responsive to the divine that God can be said to dwell in him in a way quite different from the way he dwells in even the most saintly of human beings. But *how* full divinity and full humanity form a unity in Christ, the Antiochenes could not say: they had various theories and analogies, but their concern was to emphasize the distinctness and integrity of the two natures of Christ, as it was important for them that the humanity of Christ still functioned with full human integrity, since on that our redemption depended.

The first stage of this final Christological conflict was fought out between Cyril and Nestorius, and culminated in the Council of Ephesus (431) at which Nestorius was condemned, deposed as patriarch of Constantinople, and exiled by the Emperor to the Great Oasis on the edge of the Libyan desert. Nestorianism (as the heresy of the Antiochenes was called) was condemned for dissolving the unity of Christ, as, in effect, preaching 'two Sons' (a charge Nestorius always denied).

It was the second stage of the conflict that resulted in the Council of Chalcedon. Nestorius was still in exile, his successor Proclus was dead and had been succeeded by Flavian; in Alexandria, Cyril had died and his successor was Dioscorus. In Constantinople an aged monk of great sanctity, and considerable influence at the imperial court, an archimandrite (head of a monastery) called Eutyches, began to insist that the true teaching about Christ, the teaching of the great Cyril, must be expressed by saying 'one nature after the union'; and further, that this one nature of Christ was not 'of one substance with us'. Christ was God in human form, that was the important thing.

Flavian censured Eutyches; Eutyches appealed to Dioscorus, who with some of his bishops set sail for Ephesus to support Eutyches against this 'new Nestorius'. At a synod held in Ephesus in 449, Eutyches was upheld and Flavian condemned (and so ill-treated that he soon died). Flavian had appealed to Rome, to Pope Leo, who had given him his support in a letter, the famous 'Tome of Leo', which condemned Eutyches and set out Leo's teaching on Christology. More important for the immediate course of events, the Emperor Theodosius II died and was succeeded by Marcian, who married the widowed Empress Pulcheria, who became the real power behind the throne. Pulcheria's sympathies were with Flavian and Leo, and a new council was called, which eventually met at Chalcedon in 451. The Council deposed Dioscorus for his part in the Synod of Ephesus (called by Leo the *Latrocinium*, the 'Robber Synod'), rehabilitated Flavian (posthumously: he was now dead and had been succeeded by Anatolius), and proceeded to draw up a definition of Faith.

The Chalcedonian Definition begins by reaffirming the creed of the Council of Nicaea and the creed of the Council of Constantinople, and then endorsing the teaching of Cyril, as expressed in various of his letters, and the teaching of Leo, as put forth in his 'Tome'. Then follows the Christological definition of faith. It is cunningly constructed: based on the *Formulary of Reunion* in which Cyril and John, Bishop of Antioch from 429 to 441, had sunk their differences in 433 after the condemnation of Nestorius, it safeguards the Antiochene insistence on the integrity and distinctness of the two natures of Christ in terms drawn from the writings of Cyril (though

4

taken out of context), and sets the whole in the context of an Alexandrine emphasis on the unity of Christ. Had that been all, the Definition might have secured more acceptance than it did, but it was necessary, too, to secure the unequivocal approval of the West: the new Eastern emperor, Marcian, needed the approval of the Western emperor, Valentinian III. That meant not just general approval of Leo's *Tome* but the incorporation into the Definition of its insistence that Christ exists and is known 'in two natures'. So the crucial phrase of the Definition came to read: 'One and the Same Christ, Son, Lord, Only-Begotten, known in two natures, unconfusedly, unchangeably, indivisibly, inseparably . . .'.

Far from Chalcedon settling the Christological controversy in the East, it satisfied hardly anyone. The course of the next hundred years saw a series of attempts to fashion some sort of unity out of the divided state of Eastern Christendom. For many Christians, Chalcedon seemed to represent a betrayal of Cyril and the Council of Ephesus. Had they known, they would not have been surprised to learn that the aged Nestorius, in exile at the Oasis, had welcomed the news of Leo's support for Flavian in his *Tome* as a vindication of himself. Leo's insistence on the separateness of the two natures in their activities—'the property of each nature is preserved as they unite in one person', 'each form performs what is proper to it in communion with the other . . . one of them flashes forth in miracles, the other succumbs to injuries'—seemed to open the door to Nestorianism. Not that Eutyches found much support for his idea of a Christ, one nature formed out of two, and that one nature not of one substance with us. For most of those who rejected Chalcedon rejected Eutyches, too, and insisted that while Christ formed a single nature, he was both 'of one substance with the Father' (as the Council of Nicaea had maintained) *and* 'of one substance with us' (as Cyril had maintained—and so had the *Formulary of Reunion* and, indeed, Chalcedon itself).

It was the memory of Cyril, and the fear that he had been betrayed, that fed resistance to Chalcedon in the East. Juvenal, Patriarch of Jerusalem, who had supported Dioscorus at Ephesus and had been censured at Chalcedon (though reinstated on his support for the Definition) returned to find riots in Jerusalem. Things were much the same in Syria. But it was in Egypt that the depth of resentment against Chalcedon and Leo was most apparent. Dioscorus had been exiled to Gangra, and Proterius, who had been close to Dioscorus, was appointed Patriarch in his stead. There were riots in Alexandria: the troops were called in, but were driven back and took refuge in the Serapeum, a former pagan temple, where they were burnt alive. An uneasy calm was eventually restored. But when the Emperor Marcian died in 457, Timothy Aelurus ('The Weasel', so called because of his spare physique) was elected Patriarch (Dioscorus having died in exile some time earlier) and within days Proterius had been torn to pieces by the Alexandrian mob. The Church in Egypt has never come to accept the Council of Chalcedon.

This Cyrilline reaction against Chalcedon—called 'Monophysite' (from the Greek for 'one, single, nature') by the supporters of Chalcedon, because of its rejection of the Council's phrase 'known in two natures'—commanded the hearts and minds of the East. The great names of the seventy or eighty years after Chalcedon—Timothy Aelurus, Peter Mongus ('the Hoarse'), Peter the Fuller, Philoxenus of Mabbog, Severus of Antioch, Jacob of Serugh—all rejected Chalcedon in the name of Cyril; everywhere they could call on popular support. It can, indeed, be claimed that Chalcedon only gained final acceptance by large concessions being made to the Cyrilline tradition, so that the Chalcedonian Definition came to be read in the light of the theology of the great Alexandrian.

But a divided empire, and still worse, an empire professing a standard of orthodoxy repugnant to many of its citizens, was politically intolerable. So various attempts were made to unite those who supported Chalcedon and those who rejected it. In 475 Basiliscus usurped the imperial throne. In his brief reign he issued the Encyclical which set aside Leo's *Tome* and the Council of Chalcedon and reasserted the authority of the Council of Nicaea (supplemented by the decisions of the Councils of Constantinople and Ephesus). But Basiliscus did not last long. Zeno, who reasserted his authority as Emperor in 476 and reigned until 491, attempted to achieve unity among Christians with the so-called *Henoticon* (482). This again sought to return to the authority of Nicaea (supplemented again by Constantinople and Ephesus), and has a brief Christological statement which lays emphasis on the unity of Christ, avoids any language at all of 'nature' (either one or two), and further asserts that the One who became incarnate was 'one of the Trinity, God and Word'. It thereby met the Alexandrian fear that Nestorianism introduced a fourth member into the Trinity, but (more significantly) brought into mutual relationship the doctrines of the Trinity and the incarnation in a way that foreshadowed the theological developments of the next century.

The *Henoticon* did, in fact, secure a large measure of unity in the East. It was promulgated (and composed) by Acacius, Patriarch of

Constantinople, who secured the support of Peter Mongus, Patriarch of Alexandria, and Peter the Fuller, Patriarch of Antioch (both opponents of Chalcedon, as we have seen), as well as many other bishops. But Rome, naturally, had no inclination to disavow the 'Tome of Leo', and excommunicated Acacius and those who supported him in 484. The resulting schism between East and West—the so-called Acacian schism—was only healed when, with the accession of Justin I as Emperor in 518 in the time of Pope Hormisdas, the *Henoticon* was abandoned as an instrument of unity and the way paved for the acceptance of Chalcedon.

BACK TO THE PAST

Our concern, however, is not with the details of church history, but rather to give a sketch of the theological and intellectual world of the late fifth century, which was the background of Denys the Areopagite. What is interesting about the *Henoticon* (and to a lesser extent Basiliscus's Encyclical) is not the complicated story of relations between the imperial house, the patriarchs and the bishops, and the monks and people whose confidence they needed, but the *kind* of unity that seemed attractive and attainable in the late fifth century. Both the Encyclical and the *Henoticon* lay enormous stress on the Council of Nicaea. One might wonder why: it is notorious that the Council of Nicaea itself settled nothing but merely heralded decades of arguments and councils, hardly any of which conceded Nicaea any paramount authority; on the contrary, the succession of councils constantly revising the definition of the faith of the Church only weakened the notion of conciliar authority. But from about 360 onwards, when Athanasius (and later the Cappadocian Fathers) managed to unite the Church against the extremes of Arianism, they did this in the name of the 'faith of Nicaea'. By the time of their triumph at Constantinople in 381, Nicaea had become a symbol of orthodoxy. The Councils of Constantinople, of Ephesus and indeed of Chalcedon saw themselves as reaffirming the faith proclaimed at Nicaea:

> We in no wise suffer any to unsettle the faith . . . defined by our holy Fathers assembled sometime at Nicaea. Nor assuredly do we suffer ourselves or others either to alter a phrase of what is contained therein, or to go beyond a single syllable.[4]

The Fathers[5] had no real notion of development of doctrine, and

7

little enough of any idea of history. The very newness of the Christian gospel had been an embarrassment in the early days, an embarrassment they had overcome by seeing Christ as the fulfilment of ancient prophecy, so that the newly preached Christian gospel was simply a rediscovery of what was in truth of enormous antiquity. As the Church grew and developed, the mature state of the Church was read back into the very beginnings. St Basil the Great, in the fourth century, regarded the liturgical customs of his own day as apostolic in origin,[6] something commonly insinuated by ascribing accounts of liturgical customs to the apostles: witness the *Apostolic Tradition* (early third century, ascribed to Hippolytus), and the *Canons of the Apostles*, the *Apostolic Constitutions* (both fourth century). Of course, the fourth century did see a change in the affairs of the Church: from being a persecuted minority, it became with the conversion of the Emperor Constantine in 312 the favoured religion of the Empire, and eventually the official state religion. This is presented in Eusebius' *Church History*, *par excellence*, as a rediscovery of the true state of things, which had been lost at the fall of Adam. Eusebius repeats, throughout book I, that Christianity is not 'recent and outlandish' (I.2.1) or 'new and strange' (I.4.1), but 'primitive, unique and true' (I.4.11). What was lost as a result of man's sin is restored in Christ who appeared 'in the early years of the Roman Empire' (I.2.23). As the *pax Romana* heralded the coming of the Prince of Peace, so the confession of Christ by the Roman Emperor restores everything to its original harmony: as the Word of God rules the universe, so the Emperor, in imitation of the Divine Word, rules the Empire, the *oikoumenē*.[7] The Council of Nicaea, whatever its immediate success, was a celebration of this restored state of affairs: the Christian bishops assembled at the command of the Christian emperor proclaiming the faith of the Christian Church. The enthusiasm for Nicaea in the *Henoticon* is enthusiasm for such a state of affairs.

The Peace of the Church also led to rapid liturgical development (disguised, as we have seen, by being ascribed to the apostles). The liturgy became more splendid, ceremonial took over the customs of the ceremonial of the imperial court, a conscious effort was made to provide in the liturgy a moving, symbolic, dramatic performance.[8] The whole celebration of the liturgy was surrounded by a sense of awe and mystery: only baptized Christians in good standing were allowed at the sacramental liturgy, all others (catechumens receiving instruction, Christians guilty of serious sin enrolled as penitents) were excluded from the Church after the biblical readings and the sermon. The liturgy became the focus for the encounter between God and man in Christ that is the heart of the Christian faith. Christological differences were expressed in different understandings of the liturgy. For the Antiochenes the liturgical action impressed on Christians the pattern of Christ's life of obedience and incorporated them into his humanity, his body; while for the Alexandrines, in the Eucharist the Word of God who came to be with us in the incarnation is 'again in the flesh'—in communion Christians are united with God, they are 'deified'.

Peter the Fuller, from 471 Patriarch of Antioch (though with several periods of banishment), carried the enthusiasm for doctrinal purity—understood as enthusiasm for the old teaching of Nicaea as reaffirmed by Cyril, free from the corruptions introduced by Chalcedon—into the liturgical sphere. By the use of creeds as standards of orthodoxy, Nicaea (and Constantinople) had expressed the faith in a way that could be given liturgical expression, for creeds were the summary of faith affirmed at baptism and the creeds of the councils were adopted in the baptismal liturgy (later wholesale, earlier by the incorporation of distinctive language such as 'of one substance with the Father').[9] Peter the Fuller carried this a step further: during his second period as Patriarch (475–477) he introduced the Creed into the Eucharistic liturgy, in much the same place as it occupies nowadays, between the liturgy of the word and the liturgy of the sacrament. It underlines the claim to orthodoxy on the part of those, like Peter the Fuller, who rejected Chalcedon, and expressed this orthodoxy in the words of the creed with which the Fathers at Constantinople had reaffirmed the faith of Nicaea, the so-called Niceno-Constantinopolitan Creed (still, perhaps significantly, called the 'Nicene Creed' in the Anglican *Book of Common Prayer*).[10] Peter's other liturgical innovation related to a part of the liturgy that was still a relative novelty: the so-called *Trishagion*, that is, the chant 'Holy God, Holy Strong, Holy Immortal, have mercy upon us'. First recorded in Constantinople in the time of the Patriarch Proclus (Patriarch 434–446/7), this chant had had from early days two interpretations (as had the older *Sanctus*, derived from Isaiah 6, found in the Eucharistic Prayer in most liturgies): a trinitarian and a Christological.[11] The trinitarian interpretation regarded the chant as addressed to the Trinity, as the threefold 'holy' suggests. The Christological interpretation regarded the chant as addressed to the second Person of the Trinity, the Son of God. This latter interpretation was prevalent in Syria, and the one known to Peter. To emphasize that it was indeed God himself, the Son of God,

9

who became incarnate and suffered for us—something that Cyril felt had been obscured by Nestorianism, and his supporters by the Council of Chalcedon—Peter added to the chant 'who was crucified for us', so that it now ran: 'Holy God, Holy Strong, Holy Immortal, who was crucified for us, have mercy upon us'. This shocked the Byzantine Greeks, who understood the chant as addressed to the Trinity and thus saw the addition as qualifying the impassibility of God: they accused Peter of 'theopaschitism', the doctrine that God can suffer. For Peter and those who thought like him, it simply underlined the belief that the Incarnate One was one of the Trinity, God himself: something, incidentally, affirmed in the *Henoticon*. (In the end Peter was vindicated: not that the text of the *Trishagion* was changed,[12] but the Theopaschite formula, 'One of the Trinity suffered (or, was crucified) in the flesh', was accepted as orthodox and given conciliar authority at the Second Council of Constantinople, the Fifth Ecumenical, in 553.)

THE PAST AND DENYS

The tendency to telescope the past, so that the truth now is the truth affirmed at Nicaea, itself the truth of what had been believed and suffered for during the centuries when the Church had been persecuted, was something that awakened an echo in the whole Byzantine world in a far more precise way than it would today.[13] And it is this conviction that underlies the pseudonymity adopted by our author. He was concerned with the truth, not with changeable opinion, and the truth was ancient, it was there in the very beginning. So it was under the name of one converted by St Paul himself that he wrote.[14] Our author never steps aside from his pseudonym to give us a chance to see why he adopted it: but the pseudonym of 'Dionysius the Areopagite' is very suggestive. Dionysius was the first of Paul's converts in Athens, and Athens means philosophy, and more precisely, Plato. Plato had commonly (if not quite always) been respected by Christians: the first to defend Christianity in the context of Hellenistic culture, the apologists of the second century (especially Justin Martyr), had greatly revered him, if dissenting from some of his doctrines; even the great Athanasius, the champion of orthodoxy during the Arian crisis, spoke of Plato as 'that great one among the Greeks'.[15]

The voice of Plato in Athens was not dead: the Academy he founded was still there (or so Denys would have thought: it is, however, most unlikely that it had had a continuous existence since the time of Plato) and was to remain there until the Emperor Justinian closed it in 529. For much of the fifth century the head of the Academy, the *diadochus* (the successor—of Plato), had been the great philosopher (and redoubtable pagan) Proclus. The most compelling reason for dating Denys the Areopagite to the turn of the fifth and sixth centuries is the deep sympathy that we shall see exists between the vision of Denys and the philosophy of Proclus. Denys the Areopagite, the Athenian convert, stands at the point where Christ and Plato meet. The pseudonym expressed the author's belief that the truths that Plato grasped belong to Christ, and are not abandoned by embracing faith in Christ. Both Denys and Proclus were men of their time: just as Denys saw no anachronism in speaking with the voice of a first-century Christian, so Proclus saw no anachronism in counting his elaborate speculations no more than elucidations of Plato. What appears to us a strange mongrel, the product of late Greek philosophy and a highly developed form of Christianity, appeared to Denys a pure-bred pedigree, or rather the original specimen of the species.

The great Church historian, Adolf von Harnack, dismissed the Chalcedonian Definition in these words:

> The four bald negative terms (unconfusedly, unchangeably, indivisibly, inseparably) which are supposed to express the whole truth, are in the view of the classical theologians amongst the Greeks profoundly irreligious. They are wanting in warm, concrete substance; of the bridge which his faith is to the believer, the bridge from earth to heaven, they make a line which is finer than the hair upon which the adherents of Islam one day hope to enter Paradise.[16]

There was much in the Chalcedonian Definition that caused distress, but it was hardly that. The four adverbs were drawn from Cyril of Alexandria and used by him to express the closeness of the union and the reality of the natures thus united. In using these terms, Cyril, though no professional philosopher himself, was drawing on the developing philosophical terminology of the late Platonists, such as Proclus who was fond of adding such adverbs as 'inseparably and indivisibly' when saying that two identical things were nevertheless distinct, and 'unconfusedly and unchangeably' when saying that distinguishable things are ultimately identical. Such philosophical terminology helped Cyril to affirm the mysterious unity of God and man that effected human salvation.[17]

11

Denys was fond of such language, too, but his enthusiasm for late Platonism (or Neoplatonism) went well beyond use of logical terminology: much in the deeper concerns of such philosophy attracted him. Neoplatonism is generally held to begin with the thought of the third-century philosopher Plotinus, though neither he nor his successors would have regarded themselves as innovators: they were simply Platonists. In his reflections, put together in various treatises (called the *Enneads* or the 'Nines', since they were edited by his pupil Porphyry into six books, each of nine treatises), Plotinus drew together ideas from Plato and other later thinkers into a suggestive vision.

For Plotinus, as for many of his contemporaries (and many others), multiplicity cried out for explanation and found such explanation if it could be traced back to some primordial unity. That primordial unity Plotinus called the One: everything derived from it, all beings owed their existence to a declension from original unity, or put another way were an effect of the outflow from the potent reality of the ultimacy of the One. Closest to the One was the realm of Intellect, which corresponds to Plato's realm of the Forms or Ideas, where there is true knowledge of differentiated reality. Beyond that is the realm of Soul, which is still further from the unity of the One, where knowledge is only the result of searching, and Soul itself is distracted by its lack of unity. Beyond the soul is the material order which receives what coherence it has from the realm of Soul. Beyond that there is nothing, for such disintegration has itself no hold on being.

This outward movement of progressively diminishing radiation from the One, called 'procession' or 'emanation', is met by a movement of yearning on the part of all beings for unity, or—which comes to the same thing—for return to the One. Such return is a spiritual movement towards deeper inwardness, a movement of recollection, fostered by and expressed in contemplation.

Such a way of understanding reality answers two problems: on the one hand, it suggests a way of looking at the interrelatedness of everything; on the other, it answers the spiritual problem of how to cope with our sense of being disorientated, at odds with ourselves and other people, out of touch with the roots of our being. Plotinus's insights were developed in various ways by his successors: all that really concerns us is the form they took in the late Athenian Neoplatonism that Denys found so congenial. For us that means Proclus, as little else has survived, though it is very likely that Denys knew much that is now lost to us.

Media-
tion

One theme in Plotinus is particularly important to Proclus, and that is the theme of mediation. Fundamental to Plotinus is his desire to relate the One and the many: the deepest problems in Plotinus's philosophy are due to the fact that *any* movement from the One takes one *immediately* to the many. Nevertheless Plotinus seeks to disguise the abruptness of this move by various mediating devices, especially perhaps that of distinguishing between the One as the First Number, and the One as the source of everything else, including number. For Proclus this very problem of mediation is the hinge of his philosophy: and because to relate two things is to invoke a third that mediates, his philosophy comes to abound in triads. These triads link everything together. Reality itself has a threefold structure: the One, Intellect, and Soul, of Plotinus. Any level of reality, once it admits of differentiation, lays bare a threefold structure: being, life and intelligence. These triads are not a static classification, but express a movement that pulsates through everything, a movement expressed in the triad: rest, procession and return. Reality, arranged in levels that mediate and relate one to another, takes the form of 'hierarchies' (the term is Denys's, but the concept is there in Proclus). These hierarchies express the graded levels of reality, all of which link up with one another through a cosmic sympathy that embraces the whole.

For Plotinus all this was on the one hand a logical and metaphysical analysis of reality, and on the other an elucidation of the way in which the soul can return to Intellect and thence to the One by a movement of contemplation and purification culminating in ecstatic union. But such a movement of return by contemplation is open only to very few: Plotinus's successors sought some other way by which this movement of return could be made accessible to a less restricted group. Increasingly they put their trust in an attempt to release the power of higher divine beings by the ceremonies of ancient paganism—sacrifice, divination and such-like—so that divine assistance could make up for the frailty of ordinary human effort. Such tapping of divine power was called 'theurgy' (a word coined, it would seem, in the late second century AD).[18] Iamblichus's work *On the Mysteries of Egypt*, from the first half of the fourth century, is a full-scale treatise on theurgy, and Proclus himself says that theurgy is 'better than any human wisdom or knowledge'.[19]

This is the world of Denys the Areopagite: both the Christian world of the late fifth century, marked by opposition or indifference to Chalcedon, but deeply convinced of the divine presence in Christ,

Denys's reality

and the pagan world of late Athenian Neoplatonism. Like Proclus, Denys's vision of reality abounds in triads: from the Trinity itself, through the ranks of the angels, arranged three by three, down to the threefold ministry of bishops, priests and deacons that ministers to the Christian community, itself arranged in threes. His metaphysical analysis of reality is also marked by Procline triads, as is his understanding of man's ascent to the divine. He is also fond of the vocabulary of late Neoplatonism: his use of the word 'theurgy' in relation to the Christian sacraments is but one example. We shall see, however, that though his language and categories are inconceivable except against the background of Procline Neoplatonism, his thought is distinctive; and often pagan Neoplatonic themes are turned on their head. This is true of his doctrine of creation and the oneness of God, which he sets over against a doctrine of procession and what he regards as a related polytheism; and also of his understanding of the sacraments.

But Denys belongs equally, in a somewhat elusive way, to the Christian world of the late fifth century. Scholars are still divided as to whether his Christology is 'Monophysite': it seems most likely that his language has something of the deliberate ambiguity of the *Henoticon*. But his idea that in the incarnation what is beyond being (namely God) takes on being in the person of Jesus, seems to express in his own peculiar language a Cyrilline way of speaking of the incarnation.[20] His stress on deification (Christian, not pagan, language) likewise fits such a context. So it is not surprising that he is first mentioned in Christian history when, at a colloquy held between supporters of Chalcedon and supporters of Severus of Antioch in 532, a passage from the fourth Epistle is (mis-)quoted in support of the Severian, Monophysite, position. One particular detail seems to place him firmly in this world, and that occurs in his account of the liturgy in the *Ecclesiastical Hierarchy*. There he seems to envisage the singing of the Creed in the middle of the liturgy, something which, as we have seen, was only introduced by Peter the Fuller at Antioch, probably in 476.[21] This confirms that Denys was writing at the turn of the fifth and sixth centuries, and in Syria, which fits with everything else we know about him.

Notes

1 See esp. Koch, *Ps-Dionysius*; *idem*, 'Proklus als Quelle des Ps-Dionysius Areopagita in der Lehre von Bösen', *Philologus* 54/1 (Neue Folge, 8/1; 1895), pp. 438–54; J. Stiglmayr, 'Der Neuplatoniker Proclus als Vorlage des sog. Dionysius Areopagita in der Lehre vom Übel', *Historisches Jahrbuch* 16 (1895), pp. 253–73, 721–48. On the earlier history of doubts about the authenticity of CA, see I. Hausherr, 'Doutes au sujet du "Divin Denys" ', *Orientalia Christiana Periodica* 2 (1936), pp. 484–90.

2 For perhaps the last attempt to defend the traditional legend, see J. Parker, *The Celestial and Ecclesiastical Hierarchies of Dionysius the Areopagite* (London, 1894), pp. 1–14.

3 See Roques, *Structures*, pp. 74–115.

4 Cyril, Ep. 39 (108C–D).

5 The word 'Fathers' is, in fact, an example of this kind of reverence for the past. The term, applied to past orthodox teachers of the Christian faith, is first used in the third century. It later comes to mean (and is still used to mean) the orthodox teachers of the formative years of the Christian tradition: a flexible period, usually spanning the first seven or eight centuries, sometimes stretching as far as the twelfth (St Bernard in the West) or the fourteenth (St Gregory Palamas in the East). The passage from the Council of Ephesus, just quoted, invokes the 'Holy Fathers', and the Chalcedonian Definition begins with the expression, 'Following therefore the Holy Fathers . . .'. See the articles by G. Florovsky, reprinted as chs 6 and 7 in *Bible, Church and Tradition: an Eastern Orthodox View* (Belmont, MA, 1972), pp. 93–120.

6 Basil, *On the Holy Spirit* XXVII.66.

7 Eusebius, *Oration on the Tricennalia of Constantine* 2.1–5.

8 See E. J. Yarnold, *The Awe-Inspiring Rites of Initiation* (Slough, 1972).

9 On this see J. N. D. Kelly, *Early Christian Creeds* (3rd ed., London, 1972), pp. 323–5, 344–8.

10 Ibid., pp. 348–51.

11 On this whole question, see Sebastian Brock, 'The thrice-holy hymn in the liturgy', *Sobornost'/Eastern Christian Review* 7:2 (1985), pp. 24–34.

12 See John Damascene, *Expositio Fidei* III.10 (54) (ed. B. Kotter, Berlin and New York, 1973, pp. 129–31).

13 See Norman Baynes's lecture 'The Hellenistic civilization and East Rome', repr. in *Byzantine Studies and Other Essays* (London, 1955), pp. 1–23.

14 On the question of Denys's pseudonym, see Hans Urs von Balthasar, *The Glory of the Lord*, vol. 2 (Eng. trans., .Edinburgh, 1984), pp. 148–51.

15 Athanasius, *On the Incarnation* 2.

16 A. von Harnack, *History of Dogma* IV (Eng. trans., London, 1898), pp. 222f.

17 See Ruth M. Siddals, 'Logic and Christology in Cyril of Alexandria', *Journal of Theological Studies* 38 (1987), pp. 341–67.

18 On theurgy, see H. Lewy, *Chaldaean Oracles and Pagan Theurgy* (rev. ed. by M. Tardieu, Paris, 1978), esp. *excursus* iv, pp. 461–6; E. R. Dodds, 'Theurgy', Appendix ii in *The Greeks and the Irrational* (Berkeley, CA, 1951), pp. 283–311.

19 *Platonic Theology* I.25 (ed. H. D. Saffrey and L. G. Westerink, Paris, 1968: p. 113).

20 See Ep. 4.

21 EH III.ii: 425D; III.iii.7: 436C–D.

2

A liturgical theology

THE WORKS OF DENYS

The works of the Areopagitical Corpus consist of four treatises and ten letters (though the distinction is somewhat artificial in that all the works are addressed to specific people, and two of the letters—Epp. VIII and IX—are each longer than one of the treatises, the *Mystical Theology*). The four treatises (all addressed to Timothy, a bishop, doubtless to be understood as the correspondent of St Paul) are the *Celestial Hierarchy*, the *Ecclesiastical Hierarchy*, the *Divine Names*, and the *Mystical Theology*. The first four letters are addressed to a monk called Gaius; Ep. V to a deacon, Dorotheus; Ep. VI to a priest, Sosipater; Ep. VII to a bishop, Polycarp (doubtless the Bishop of Smyrna: the account of his martyrdom is the earliest such account to survive;[1] he was reputed to be a disciple of the apostle John and a friend of Ignatius, Bishop of Antioch, who was martyred at the beginning of the second century[2] and whom Denys once quotes[3]); Ep. VIII to a monk, Demophilus; Ep. IX to a bishop, Titus (presumably the other recipient of St Paul's pastoral epistles); and Ep. X to the apostle John. Where his correspondents are identifiable, their names serve to establish Denys's pseudonym: they suggest that he was writing at the end of the first or beginning of the second century. This is further borne out by his mentioning, as contemporaries, other people known from the New Testament, or the early history of the Church: for example, Elymas the magician (DN VIII.6; cf. Acts 13:8) and Carpus (Ep. VIII; cf. 2 Tim 4:13). But they do more than establish Denys's pseudonymity, they also present him as part of a *society*. Denys does not present himself to the world simply as the author of various treatises: he presents himself as a member of a society, bound and defined by relationships. This consciousness of belonging to an ordered society is further underlined by the order of the letters: addressed to holders of the office of monk, deacon, priest, bishop, and apostle, in that order, with the exception of Ep. VIII which is addressed to a monk, though between letters written to bishops—but that break in hierarchical sequence has its own significance, since it is concerned to rebuke a monk who usurped the role of a priest. A society, an ordered ecclesiastical society, within which one member turns to another for advice and counsel, in which there are teachers and disciples, venerated holy men, propounders of false teaching and raisers of objections, in which there is a regular cycle of prayer and worship: that is the society Denys reflects in his writings, and of which he seems very fond. And we should admit straight away that it is a somewhat limited conception of society. There is no mention of the everyday world of work and play, nor is there any mention of political authority. It is an ecclesiastical, even a monastic society. But it is nonetheless a society: the Dionysian writings are not a collection of academic treatises concerned simply with ideas and concepts.

That is an important point to grasp, since, too often, in the history of Christian thought (especially in the West) they have been taken to be just that. In the Western Middle Ages, the *Divine Names* was regarded as a treatise discussing what properties may be said to pertain to God, and the *Mystical Theology* was taken to concern the rare case of mystical experience of God; the works on the hierarchies fell into the background, though the *Celestial Hierarchy* was valued for the information it gave on the structure of the realm of the angels and the *Ecclesiastical Hierarchy* for its useful hints on sacramental causality. This way of treating Denys has continued to the present day, so that Denys is thought of primarily as a philosopher or a mystic. It may be that the real core of what Denys is trying to say *is* philosophical, but that is not how he presents his writings. They are intended to serve the needs of a Christian community, and the immediate object of his concern is the use of the Christian Scriptures within that community. One of his treatises, the *Divine Names*, is concerned with the meaning of various scriptural terms for God; another, the *Celestial Hierarchy*, is concerned with the meaning of imagery drawn from the realm of the senses and applied, by the Scriptures, to the immaterial realm (of the angels) where the revelation of the Supreme Godhead is first manifest; the *Ecclesiastical Hierarchy* is concerned to expound and interpret the ceremonies of

18

the Church. Of the letters, four of them elucidate specific scriptural usages, and one, Ep. IX, is virtually a short treatise on the interpretation of the Scriptures.

THE LOST WORKS

If, then, we are going to take Denys at his own word, at least to begin with, we should recognize that his immediate concern is with the meaning of the Scriptures; not, again, as an abstract academic matter of theological hermeneutics, but quite concretely, with the meaning of the Scriptures as they are used in the Christian community, especially in its worship.

If we are going to take Denys seriously, there is, however, another point we must note. The four treatises and ten letters are not the only writings to which Denys lays claim. In the *Divine Names*, he refers to five other works: the *Theological Outlines, On the Properties and Ranks of the Angels, On the Soul, On Righteous and Divine Judgement*, and the *Symbolic Theology*. The *Mystical Theology* in its summary of theological method (in ch. III) presents the *Theological Outlines, Divine Names*, and *Symbolic Theology* as three successive treatises. The *Celestial Hierarchy* refers back to the *Symbolic Theology* and mentions a work *On the Divine Hymns*. The *Ecclesiastical Hierarchy* refers back to the *Celestial Hierarchy* and mentions another work, *The Intelligible and the Sensible*. Ep. IX again refers back to the *Symbolic Theology*. On the one hand, this suggests that the order of composition of the treatises that we have is DN, MT, CH, and EH, which is the order in which they are printed in the new translation by Luibheid and Rorem (and in the older French translation by Maurice de Gandillac).[4] In the manuscripts of the Areopagitical Corpus the order is CH, EH, DN, MT, Epp.: we shall come back to this point later.

On the other hand, all this presents us with a problem: what has happened to the seven treatises Denys mentions that have not survived? And how important are they for an understanding of Dionysian theology? Opinions about this vary among scholars. Hans Urs von Balthasar takes Denys quite seriously here and supposes that the missing treatises were written (or sketched out, at least in his mind); he works out the structure of Dionysian theology taking account, in principle, of all the works mentioned.[5] However, there is no trace at all of these 'lost' treatises: despite the interest in Denys from as early as the sixth century, no mention of them is to be found. Added to that, there is no trace of two other works Denys refers to and quotes from: the *Hymns of Love* and the *Elements of Theology* of the one he regarded as his mentor, Hierotheus. Such a silence in the tradition makes one wonder whether the missing treatises are not fictitious, conjured up to give the impression, perhaps, that the works we have were all that survived to the end of the fifth century of a much larger corpus of writings written at the end of the first.[6]

Mystical Theology III gives a brief account of theological method and speaks of a theology that traces the movement down from God through the successive manifestations of himself to the material and sensible order, a movement that is followed in the three treatises: the *Theological Outlines*, which treats of the doctrines of the Trinity and the incarnation; the *Divine Names*, which discusses how goodness, being, life, wisdom and power are ascribed to God; and the *Symbolic Theology*, which considers the use of images drawn from the material world when applied to God. These Denys calls *cataphatic* theologies (that is, concerned with affirmation), and contrasts them with *apophatic* theologies (that is, concerned with negation), which he does not name and which seem to trace the corresponding movement of return, or ascent from the material to the divine. If we look from this to the work which is called the *Divine Names*, we see that DN I–II correspond to the *Theological Outlines*, and are perhaps a summary of it, while the rest of DN corresponds to what the *Mystical Theology* says it contains. Ep. IX says that it is a summary of part of the *Symbolic Theology*, and the *Celestial Hierarchy* (especially ch. XV) covers the same kind of ground as that work. This suggests that the 'loss' of the 'missing' treatises is not as serious as it first seems, since here—the one place where Denys makes any attempt to explain the relationship between his writings, even though only one out of three of the treatises mentioned survives—we can reasonably well make out from what we do have what his system contains.[7]

A CHRISTIAN AND A NEOPLATONIST

The chapter in the *Mystical Theology* we have briefly looked at brings out another point: that though Denys's intention may be to expound the Christian Scriptures, underlying his theological method are assumptions of a rather different provenance. For the movement of theology that Denys envisages clearly presupposes the Neoplatonic idea of corresponding movements of procession (or emanation) and return: cataphatic theology seems to trace the movement of procession, a movement from oneness to multiplicity; apophatic theology traces the corresponding movement of return, moving from multiplicity closer and closer to oneness, until one passes into 'the darkness beyond understanding' and is reduced to 'complete speechlessness and failure of understanding'.

This raises one of the fundamental questions about Denys the Areopagite: the relationship between Christianity and Neoplatonism in his thought. One thing, however seems quite clear. Denys' writings are *explicitly* Christian. It is the Christian Scriptures that he seeks to interpret in his writings, not the works of Plato or the Chaldaean Oracles (a source of supposedly 'revealed' wisdom much beloved of later Neoplatonists, such as Proclus). When he quotes, he quotes from the Scriptures. He never ascribes any authority to (pagan) Greek philosophical sources.

On the other hand, it is undeniable that many of his concepts are derived from Neoplatonism. We have just seen an example of the way he understands theological method against the background of the Neoplatonic doctrine of procession and return. Elsewhere he echoes much that is at home in the metaphysics of Proclus: we mentioned several of the more obvious points at the end of the last chapter—three levels of reality corresponding to the One, Intellect and Soul, his use of Proclus's analysis of reality into the triad, being–life–intelligence (the last lightly 'Christianized' as wisdom). But Denys's sympathy with Neoplatonism goes much further, and much deeper. If he never quotes from Plato and the Neoplatonists, he frequently *alludes* to them. In DN II.7 on love of the beautiful, he reproduces word for word part of Diotima's speech to Socrates from the *Symposium* (211A–B). It is not a quotation only because he does not say where it comes from. His allusions to the *Timaeus* are particularly frequent. He is very fond of words from Platonic dialogues or the Chaldaean Oracles that one would never expect to find in a Christian, but would regard as commonplace in a pagan philosopher. All this has been demonstrated by scholars and is undeniable.[8]

A particular example will bring out points that are typical. In Ep. VIII, Denys concludes his exhortation to the erring monk, Demophilus, by giving a moving account of a vision that a monk, Carpus, had once had. The vision was a rebuke to Carpus who had allowed his feeling of righteous anger to lead him to pray for the destruction of a couple of sinners. In the vision Carpus sees on high, 'in the vault of heaven', Jesus surrounded by the angels; but below he sees the two sinners trembling on the edge of a chasm that opens on to the depths of hell whence serpents and evil men seek to force

21

and entice the men to tumble down among them. Carpus finds the plight of the men fascinating and is only sorry that they do not fall into the pit more quickly. Then he looks up and sees Jesus again, going down to the men to stop them from falling. Jesus turns to Carpus and says, 'You were going to strike them. Strike me instead. I would gladly suffer again for men if by doing so I could stop other men from sinning.' It is a telling illustration of the gentle endurance that Denys sees as characteristic of the love of God. There is a very similar account of such a vision granted to a monk called Carpus preserved in Greek monastic literature under the name of Nilus, dating from the fifth century.[9] It is conceivably the source of Denys's account. The contrasts are instructive: Nilus does not make out that Carpus was his contemporary, whereas Denys does; and Nilus's account is innocent of the Platonic allusions that we find in Denys. Denys's account is redolent of the myth of Er from the *Republic*, book X; the 'many-coloured flames' are from there, the 'vault of heaven' from the *Phaedrus* (247C). Carpus's vision occurs at midnight, the holy hour when men see visions, by Denys's account. He has both made the account subserve his pseudonymity, and also given it a much more distinctively Platonic colouring.[10]

Even his attitude to the Scriptures is given a 'pagan' colouring. He hardly ever uses the Christian word (*graphē*), but prefers to refer to them as 'oracles' (*logia*), using the word pagans used. He also, in Ep. IX, presents a picture of the absurdity of the literal meaning of the Scriptures that it would be hard to find in any other Christian Father: it sounds much more like a pagan Greek apologizing for the absurdities of the Greek myths:

> Viewed from outside they seem full of so many incredible and fictitious fairy-tales. So, for example, in the case of the coming-to-be of God [the theogony] that is beyond being, they imagine the womb of God bodily giving birth to God, or the Word poured forth into the air from a human heart which sends it out, or they describe the Spirit as breath breathed out of a mouth, or the theogonic bosom embracing the Son: all this we celebrate in forms befitting bodily things, and we depict these things with images drawn from nature, suggesting a certain tree, and plants, and flowers, and roots, or fountains gushing forth water, or sources of light radiating beams of light, or certain other sacred forms used by the Scriptures to expound divine matters beyond being. In the matter of the intelligible providences of God, or His gifts, or manifestations,

powers, properties, fortunes, abodes, processions, distinctions, and unions, the human imagination applies to God a variety of forms found among beasts and other living things and plants and stones, and arrays Him with feminine ornaments and barbarian armour and with ornaments of ceramic and metalwork, as if he were a mere artisan. It supplies Him with horses and chariots and thrones, and provides delicately prepared banquets and depicts Him drinking, and drunk, and drowsy, and suffering from a hangover. And what about God's fits of anger, His griefs, His various oaths, His moments of repentance, His curses, His wraths, the manifold and crooked reasons given for His failure to fulfil promises? And the battle of the giants [the *gigantomachia*] in Genesis, when God is said to have taken counsel out of fear of the power of those men who were building the tower not in order to injure others, but for their own safety, or that plot fashioned in heaven to deceive Ahab by a trick? What about the variety of sensual passions, passions appropriate to a prostitute, described in the Song of Songs, and all the other sacred signs that are daringly used to manifest God and to protect what is hidden, and make manifold and divided what is single and indivisible, and give a variety of form and figure to what is without form or figure? (1104D–1105C)

There is nothing new about a Christian theologian in the fifth century advocating allegory, but Denys's eagerness to jettison the literal meaning of Scripture, and his willingness to see unsavoury views of the divine there, is unusual, or at least extreme.

What is one to make of this mixture of Christianity and Neoplatonism? Is the Christianity simply a cover for his real conviction which is pagan Neoplatonism? Is he perhaps trying to find within Christianity a place where a now-outlawed Platonism can continue to survive?[11] The long answer to that—for my part—is the rest of this book, which hopes to show that what Denys expounds in his writings is recognizably Christian. The immediate answer, or the beginnings of such, is to note that by the end of the fifth century educated Greek Christians and pagan philosophers had much in common, because they *shared a culture*. Even in the West in the fifth and sixth centuries, there were educated men whose Christianity was expressed in the clothing of a pagan culture to such an extent that one wonders what their real allegiance was: one thinks of Sidonius Apollinaris or of Boethius. We recognize them as belonging to a dying culture,

23

because Western (pagan) culture did die and yielded to a 'Christian' culture. But the fate of Greek culture was different: the Empire did not collapse, secular education continued; as late as the eleventh century (Michael Psellus) or even the fourteenth (Gemistos Plethon), there were Greeks whose real allegiance seems doubtful. In Denys's time this common culture meant that many terms and expressions had a meaning and a life in both a pagan and a Christian context. Earlier scholars argued that for Denys such words as 'theologian', 'theology', and 'tradition' were used not in a Christian but in a Neoplatonic way. They were right that Denys's use of these words is not much different from the way Neoplatonists used them: but Christians and Neoplatonists did, by this time, use these terms in very similar ways.

We saw in the last chapter that Cyril of Alexandria had picked up from Neoplatonic logic notions like 'inseparable union' and 'unconfused distinction' and that these eventually found their way into the Chalcedonian Definition. Given that, it is hopeless to say, as some scholars have, that Denys's use of such language is reminiscent rather of Neoplatonism than of Chalcedon. The distinction between Christian and pagan in the fifth century was not so much a matter of language or method, as we are tempted to view it when we regard commitment to a philosophy such as Platonism as inimical to real Christianity; rather it was a matter of the convictions expressed through language and by means of whatever methods were to hand. It is the substance of Denys's convictions we need to examine. We should not assume that what he says is wholly conditioned by the way he delights in saying it. Denys may be more sensitive or more clearheaded than we might suppose possible.

THE NATURE OF THEOLOGY

In several places Denys talks directly about the nature of theological language. One such passage occurs in Ep. IX. There Denys says,

> that the tradition of the theologians is twofold, on the one hand ineffable and mystical, on the other manifest and more knowable; on the one hand symbolic and presupposing initiation, on the other philosophical and capable of proof—and the ineffable is interwoven with what can be uttered. The one persuades and contains within itself the truth of what it says, the other effects and establishes the soul with God by initiations that do not teach anything. (1105D)

We have on the one hand, then, what appears to be a rational theological method which works openly, using philosophical means, persuading by means of proof and making the truth available to us; on the other hand, we have another tradition which is concerned with what is unknowable and unutterable, which is only open to the initiate, employs symbolism and by some kind of action puts the soul securely in contact with God without teaching anything. This contrast recalls the contrast Plato made between philosophy which is expressed in terms of *logos* (reason) and is capable of proof, and teaching which is handed down in the form of myth (*mythos*). It recalls even more vividly what Aristotle said about the Eleusinian mysteries, that there the initiates do not learn (*mathein*) anything, rather they experience (*pathein*, or suffer) something:[12] Denys's second type of theology, reserved only for initiates, is said explicitly not to teach anything. Both these distinctions, and others, are made use of by Neoplatonist philosophers, Proclus, for example.[13] The contrast between learning and suffering (which in Greek involves a play on words: *mathein—pathein*) is used elsewhere by Denys, when he speaks of his master, Hierotheus. The teaching of Hierotheus consisted of

whatever he learned directly from the sacred writers, whatever his own perspicacious and laborious research of the scriptures uncovered for him, or whatever was made known to him through that more mysterious inspiration, not only learning (*mathōn*) but also experiencing (*pathōn*) the divine things. For he had a 'sympathy' with such matters, if I may express it this way, and he was perfected in a mysterious union with them and in a faith in them which was independent of any teaching. (DN II.9)

Denys clearly regards Hierotheus as an adept at his second, more mysterious kind of theology. But what kind of an adept was he? Traditionally he has been taken to be some kind of experiential mystic, who experiences God and does not just know about him. That his knowledge of God was based on experience and not some more indirect source is evident, but whether it is the individual experience of the mystic (maybe of some ecstatic kind) that is involved is not so clear. The answer to that will depend, to some extent, on the importance for Denys of such 'mystical' experience: something we shall have to discuss later. But the experience that Aristotle had in mind when he spoke of the Eleusinian mysteries was certainly not of any such kind: he meant that the initiate learnt nothing but simply underwent an experience (of the rite of initiation). Denys, too, seems to be speaking of the experience of a rite or ceremony when he speaks of the theology of the initiate, expressed in symbolism, for he goes on to speak of the use of symbolism in the 'rites of the most holy mysteries' both in the Church of the Old Testament and that of the New, and of the angels' use of riddles to introduce divine mysteries, and of 'Jesus himself, speaking of divine matters in parables, and passing on to us the mysteries of his divine activity through the symbolism of a meal laid out on a table' (Ep. IX: 1108A). It does not seem to be the experience of mystical rapture that Denys has in mind, but the experience of Christian liturgical worship.

There is another problem in taking Denys's distinction of two kinds of theology in Ep. IX as referring to a distinction between rational theology and some sort of mystical, experiential theology, and that is that though Denys's language seems to suggest that the first kind of theology is rational and philosophical, that cannot be really what he means; for the distinction occurs *within* 'the tradition of the theologians', and that expression—'the tradition of the theologians'—as Denys understands it, completely excludes any kind of simply rational, philosophical theology, as we (and even Plato) would understand it. 'Tradition' for Denys means something handed down from the past—he is not at all interested in what we can discover for ourselves by the exercise of our native wit (Hierotheus's 'perspicacious and laborious research' is applied to the Scriptures); and 'theologians' does not for Denys mean learned academics, nor even sacred teachers in general, but it refers quite specifically to the biblical writers: Moses, the prophets, the evangelists, the apostles. So the two kinds of theology Denys has in mind are to be found within the tradition of biblical theology, as he understood it.

Perhaps the nearest parallel to Denys's distinction here is to be found, not in the pagan philosophical tradition that meant so much to him, but in the Christian theological tradition that he was heir to. In his work *On the Holy Spirit*, St Basil the Great makes a distinction within the teaching of the Church between *dogma* and *kērygma*, doctrine and proclamation. *Kērygma* (plural: *kērygmata*) is based on written teaching, *dogmata* are based on the tradition of the apostles which has been handed down secretly ('in a mystery'). Both, he says, have an equal claim on our reverence. If one ignores the *dogmata*, one would evacuate the Church's preaching, the *kērygmata*, of meaning. The examples that Basil gives of *dogmata* are the meanings behind various liturgical customs: the sign of the cross, prayer facing East, the words used in the Eucharistic Prayer to consecrate the sacred elements of bread and wine, the blessing of the water of baptism, the oil of anointing, the words used at the rite of baptism itself, the triple immersion, and so on. All this, Basil says, is based on no written tradition, on no Scripture, but it is based on a

> teaching kept private and secret which our holy fathers have preserved in a silence that prevents anxiety and curiosity . . . so as to safeguard by this silence the sacred character of the mysteries. The uninitiate are not permitted to behold these things: their meaning is not to be divulged by being written down.

Basil goes on to say that the same principle of safeguarding what is sacred was employed by Moses in his planning of the Temple, and by the 'apostles and the Fathers' in their regulations concerning Christian worship. He adds that the obscurity which envelops the Scriptures and makes it difficult to grasp the teaching they contain is a 'form of silence'.[14] Basil's distinction between *kērygma* and *dogma* seems then to amount to this: *kērygma* is the Church's preaching of the gospel, it is something proclaimed, it seeks to awaken faith in those who do not believe, it seeks to persuade, to convert; *dogma*, on the other hand, is the experience of the mystery of Christ within the bosom of the Church, which is to be kept secret from those outside, from those who do not have faith—it is a growing understanding of the faith mediated through the experience of the liturgy of the Church and a deeper grasp of the hidden significance of the Scriptures. This distinction seems very close to Denys's 'twofold tradition of the theologians'. The hidden, inner dimension of theology is a matter of experience, but not (or not necessarily) a matter of extraordinary, ecstatic experience (we shall have something to say later about Denys's understanding of ecstasy): it is a matter of a lifetime's experience of prayer and worship within the bosom of the Church. The inner riches of the mystery of the faith are continually being unfolded: Basil goes on to say that 'a whole day would not suffice to expound the unwritten mysteries of the Church'.[15] It is presented in the liturgy in the form of symbolism: the symbolism of the ceremonies and gestures of the liturgical rite, the symbolism of the material elements used—water, bread, wine, oil, incense, the colours of the vestments, and so on—and the symbolism of the language of the Scriptures read, and perhaps even more importantly of the songs sung during the liturgy (one of Denys's 'lost works' is *On the Divine Hymns*).

27

HIEROTHEUS

It is in this context that we should understand Hierotheus. Denys refers to him several times as his revered teacher or guide (*kathēgemōn*): one presumes that he was a bishop, or at least a priest.[16] Twice he speaks of his visions (DN II.9, III.2), and several times he refers to him for particular details of Christian teaching: for example, the idea that the angels are ranked in three triads (CH VI.2), or the dignity of the Eucharist as the 'rite of rites' (EH III.i). We have seen that it is probably misleading to describe him as a mystic. But it is not so much because such *language* is inappropriate, as because we tend to give it a meaning that is anachronistic when applied to Hierotheus by Denys. For the word 'mystic' does have a use in the Dionysian writings, which bears very closely on Hierotheus's importance for Denys.

Behind the words 'mystic', 'mysticism', lies the Greek root, *mu-*, suggesting something closed: the group of words derived from it—*mystikos, mystērion, mystēs*—were used in connection with the Greek mystery religions. The use of such language quickly became little more than a stylistic device to underline the idea that truth is hard of access, less something discovered than something disclosed: such use of this language goes back to Parmenides and Plato. The Christian use of this vocabulary really stems from the Pauline use of the word *mystērion*. *Mystērion* means a secret, but in its use in the New Testament it has a very specific reference, to the mystery of God's love for mankind revealed in Christ. It is a secret, or a mystery, not because it is kept secret; on the contrary, it is something to be proclaimed and made known. But since it is a matter of the revealing of *God's* love for mankind, it is the revelation of something that remains hidden in its revealing, inexhaustible and inaccessible in the very event of its being made known and accessible to us in the life, death and resurrection of Christ. So in Christian vocabulary, *mystikos* means something that refers us to this mystery of God's love for us in Christ and makes it accessible to us. Thus it comes to have three ranges of meaning: first, refering to a 'mystic', or hidden, meaning of Scripture; secondly, referring to the 'mystic', or inner, meaning of the sacraments (or 'mysteries', as they are called in Greek); and thirdly, 'mystical theology', knowing God as revealed in Christ, by living the life 'hid with Christ in God' (Col 3:3), by belonging to the 'fellowship of the mystery' (Eph 3:9), by living the mystery into which we are incorporated in baptism and which comes to fruition in us through the sacramental life and growth in faith, hope and love.[17] For Denys, Hierotheus exemplifies such understanding of the hidden ('mystic') truth of the Christian mystery. His experience of the Christian life is such that he has a 'sympathy' with divine matters, and thus is an expert (an experienced guide) in the hidden meaning of the Scriptures and the sacraments.

His visions fit into this context, too. The language of the second account of Hierotheus's visions (DN III.2) suggests that the context was liturgical.[18] This is supported by the fact that the other two cases of visions in CA, Carpus's in Ep. VIII and Moses' in MT I, seem to envisage a liturgical context, Carpus's explicitly and Moses' because the language that speaks of his approach to the vision is full of liturgical allusions.[19] Hierotheus's experience seems rooted in the Christian liturgy: his 'suffering divine things' (DN II.9), his 'experiencing communion with the things praised' (DN III.2) are to be understood of his celebrating the Christian sacraments. He was one who had entered into the heart of the Christian liturgy (its 'mystic' significance) and could thus explain it to others, perhaps by the very way he celebrated (hence, maybe, his being called guide, rather than simply teacher).

LITURGICAL THEOLOGY

If the heart of Denys's theology is liturgical, as all this suggests, then it perhaps explains another thing about his attitude to theology. Twice—in Epp. VI and VII—Denys warns against a polemical attitude in theology. To Sosipater he explains that a polemical argument that demolishes the opinions of an opponent does not establish anything, and, to Bishop Polycarp, he explains why he does not engage in controversy with the pagan Greeks: it is more important to expound what one holds to be true, rather than to spend one's time and energy in refuting error. There is a calmness about these two passages, a sense of serenity in the truth that is unshakable. One can imagine that if the heart of his own religious experience was the corporate experience of the Christian liturgy, this would give him a sense of sureness: the truth does not depend on his grasp of it, it has been received from the tradition, through a community which gave him, too, the support of belonging.

The two traditions of theology, Denys says, are interwoven. Even those plain and open parts of the Scripture that express the gospel to be proclaimed, the gospel of the coming of the Kingdom, or repentance, and faith in Christ—even those plain and open parts are

29

interwoven with riddles and obscurities (Jesus preached the Kingdom of God in parables) which point deeper, to the mystery we can never exhaustively understand. Similarly, however obscure and riddling the Scriptures may appear, it is never the case that to penetrate and begin to understand involves anything less than that change of mind, *metanoia*, repentance, that the gospel demands. The way in which what is plain and straightforward is bound up with what is obscure and puzzling is something that, we shall find, runs through the whole of Denys's theological work.

It is perhaps clear now why this chapter is called 'A Liturgical Theology': for it is the liturgy, and the understanding of the Scriptures that are read and expounded in the liturgy and in which the language of the liturgy is drenched, that is the fundamental context for Denys. There is a sense, a sense suggested by the categories we have seen St Basil employ, in which liturgy is more fundamental than Scripture. Basil's contrast between written and unwritten tradition, between *kērygma* and *dogma*, suggests that it is the latter that is more fundamental: *kērygma* is for everyone, *dogma* only for those who can value it. Denys echoes this distinction at the beginning of the *Ecclesiastical Hierarchy*, and contrasts the liturgy with Scripture, as being 'more immaterial' (EH I.4: 376B–C). Paul Rorem remarks that in fact Denys exaggerates the contrast between Scripture and the liturgy by emphasizing the spatial, physical and material aspects of scriptural imagery while playing down the spatial and material in the case of the liturgy—the surroundings and the objects used in the liturgy—and concentrating on 'liturgical events and ritual movements'. This bias leads to Scripture being seen as the formless expressed in the multiplicity of spatial form, and the liturgy as the timeless expressed in temporal actions. This, allied with a Platonic conviction that time is superior to space and closer to the divine—a conviction founded on the cosmology of the *Timaeus*, where time is an imitation of eternity whereas space sums up all that is contrary to the divine intention in fashioning the cosmos—completes the sense Denys conveys of the superiority of the liturgy to the Scriptures.[20]

If the liturgical is the fundamental context for Denys's theology, then it makes sense of a number of general features of his writings. That the works on the hierarchies are liturgical is clear enough, but it is no less true of the *Divine Names* and the *Mystical Theology*. The *Divine Names* is not just about the qualities we ascribe to God: it is about the names that he has given us in Scripture to call him, and we call him these names when we praise him. The *Divine Names* does not so much speak of divine predication, as divine praise: we praise or celebrate (the Greek word Denys uses is *hymnein*) God with those names that he has revealed. So the *Divine Names* is about the interpretation of the language with which we sing the praises of God. Similarly, as has already been suggested, the context of the *Mystical Theology* is not the individual 'mystic's' solitary ascent to God, but the priest's (or rather the bishop's) ascent to the altar: something that takes place with, and on behalf of, the whole people of God. So it would seem that the context of all the writings of the Areopagite is liturgical.

If we are going to approach Denys in this way, then this suggests that whoever settled the order of the treatises as found in the manuscripts—beginning with the works on the hierarchies and ending with the *Mystical Theology*—knew what he was about. Scholars may well be right in detecting another order (as we have seen), but the order in the manuscripts does introduce us to Dionysian theology in a logical and coherent way. The *Celestial Hierarchy* expounds the order and function of the angelic ranks: there we can see in an unconfused way the principles that govern hierarchical order. These principles are then applied in the *Ecclesiastical Hierarchy* to the structure and liturgy of the Church on earth (we shall see this means very much the Church that Denys was familiar with in Syria). The *Divine Names* then looks to the One who has brought all this about and whose praises we sing in the liturgy, and the *Mystical Theology* looks at the culminating significance of the liturgy and draws the whole together. We shall let this structure determine the way we shall expound the theology of the Areopagite.

Notes

1. *Martyrdom of Polycarp*, trans. in *Early Christian Writings* (Penguin Classics; rev. ed., Harmondsworth, Middx, 1987), pp. 125–35.

2. Denys himself mentions Ignatius: DN IV.12.

3. See *Early Christian Writings* (*op. cit.*), pp. 115f.

4. *Oeuvres Complètes du Pseudo-Denys l'Aréopagite*, trans. M. de Gandillac (Paris, 1943; repr. 1980). This ordering of Denys's works is not universally accepted—see G. Heil's note in his translation of the *Hierarchies* (Bibliothek der Griechischen Literatur, 23; 1986), p. 1—but is argued for by Roques, *Structures*, pp. 133f.

5. Hans Urs von Balthasar, *The Glory of the Lord* 2 (Eng. trans., Edinburgh, 1984), pp. 154–64.

6   See Roques, *Structures*, pp. 128–33 (= *Dictionnaire de Spiritualité* III (Paris, 1957), cols 259–62).

7   On the other 'lost' treatises and how we can supplement what we have 'lost' from what survives, see Balthasar, *op. cit.*

8   See, esp., Koch, *Ps-Dionysius, passim.*

9   PG 79, 297D–300C.

10 See Koch's comments, *Ps-Dionysius*, pp. 18–26.

11 As R. F. Hathaway suggests: *Hierarchy and the Definition of Order in the Letters of Pseudo-Dionysius* (The Hague, 1969), p. 25. More precisely, Hathaway thinks that the author of CA may have been Damascius, the last head of the Academy in Athens. Others who believe Denys to have been a Neoplatonist and not a Christian at all include J. Vanneste (*Le Mystère de Dieu*, Brussels, 1959), B. Brons (*Gott und die Seienden*, Göttingen, 1976), R. Mortley (*From Word to Silence* 2, ch. 12, Bonn, 1986).

12 Aristotle, *De Philosophia*, frag. 15 (Ross).

13 See Proclus's rather elaborate distinction of types of theology in the *Platonic Theology* I.4 (ed. H. D. Saffrey and L. G. Westerink, Paris, 1968, pp. 17–23).

14 Basil, *On the Holy Spirit* XXVII.66: ed. (with French trans.) B. Pruche (*Sources Chrétiennes* 17 bis, Paris, 1968), pp. 478–86.

15 Ibid., XXVII.67 (p. 486).

16 On Hierotheus, see I. P. Sheldon-Williams, 'The Pseudo-Dionysius and the holy Hierotheus', *Studia Patristica* 8 (= *Texte und Untersuchungen* 93, 1966), pp. 108–17.

17 On all this see Louis Bouyer's articles, 'Mysticism' and 'Mysterion: an essay on the history of a word' in A. Plé and others, *Mystery and Mysticism* (Blackfriars Publications; London, 1956: articles translated from *La Vie spirituelle*, Supplément, 1952); and at greater length, his book, *Mysterion: du mystère à la mystique* (Paris, 1986).

18 See Rorem's note, *Works*, p. 70, n. 131.

19 Ibid. p. 137, n. 10.

20 Rorem, *Symbols*, pp. 117–19.

3

The angelic choirs

In his work the *Celestial Hierarchy*, Denys gives an account of the realm of those heavenly, immaterial beings generally called angels. The angelic realm is represented as being closer to God than we human beings are, and thus as mediating between God and mankind. The purpose of Denys's work is partly to establish the order and rank of the angels and to give an account of their purpose. But because none of the angelic orders has any material existence, the language with which Scripture describes them is metaphorical, using imagery drawn from the realm of the senses. This raises the question about how such metaphorical language works, which is for Denys akin to the subject of symbolic theology. Descriptions of the angelic hierarchies make use of names taken from the realm of the senses and apply them to the immaterial realm which Denys calls intelligible or conceptual (in Greek: *noēton*); in symbolic theology proper names taken from the realm of the senses are applied to the divine itself.[1]

But to devote a whole treatise to the subject of angels must seem strange to modern ways of thinking: Christians still celebrate, as they have for centuries, the feasts of St Michael and All Angels (on 29 September, now called the Feast of the Archangels) and of the Holy Guardian Angels (on 2 October), and angels play a role in the Christmas stories and in the accounts of the Resurrection, but quite what they are, or whether they are at all, is not much aired.[2] In the Bible, however, angels appear a good deal. The 'angel of the Lord' in the Old Testament often seems to be a periphrasis for God: the 'angel of the Lord' is the presence of God himself (see, e.g., Judg

33

6:11–24; 13:2–23). The word 'angel' (in Greek, *angelos*; in Hebrew, *mal'ak*) means a messenger, and the angels are often depicted as messengers moving between God and men (cf., e.g., the ladder of Jacob's dream, up and down which angels passed: Gen 28:12), carrying messages from God and prayers from men. Elsewhere they are represented as a kind of heavenly court with which God consults (e.g., 1 Kings 29:19–23; Job 1:6–12); and increasingly as beings who surround God and sing his praises (Isa 6, Ps 148:2). They are the invisible company who are close to God and who support those who trust in him: holy men and women know their presence, so on one occasion, in a moment of danger, the prophet Elisha prays that his servant's eyes may be opened to see that 'those who are with us are more than those that are with them' (2 Kings 6:15–17). Already in the Old Testament there is a growing definiteness about the nature of the angelic world. As well as angels, there are seraphim (Isa 6), cherubim (guarding Paradise, Gen 3:24; in Ezekiel's vision, Ezek 10:5), and the names of some of the angelic beings are given: Michael (Dan 10:13), Gabriel (Dan 8:16) and Raphael (Tobit 7:8). These named beings were later all thought to be archangels. Belief in a body of angelic mediators who live in the presence of God singing his praises and mediating between God and men is taken for granted in the New Testament. The angel Gabriel announces to Mary her vocation as Mother of the Lord (Luke 1:26–38) and an angel tells the shepherds of the birth of Jesus (Luke 2:8–20); angels minister to Jesus in the desert (Matt 4:11) and in the Garden of Gethsemane (Luke 22:43), and announce to the women the resurrection of Jesus (Matt 28:2–7; John 20:12f.). They figure in the life of the early Church as depicted in Acts (e.g., 12:6–11), and play a prominent part in the picture of heaven found in the Apocalypse (or the book of Revelation). Such a belief in angels was commonplace in the Judaism of the day: angels were seen as mediators between God and men, in particular they were the intermediaries through whom the Law was given (a belief known to writers of the New Testament: cf., Acts 7:53, Gal 3:19, Heb 2:2). The great Jewish philosopher Philo (*c*. 20 BC – *c*. AD 50) had a highly developed angelology.

Belief in such intermediary beings was not, however, confined to the Judaeo-Christian tradition. Many people in classical and late classical times believed in such beings. In the *Symposium* (202E–204A) Plato develops the idea of a class of beings called *daemons* (Greek: *daimones*) who are intermediaries between gods and men and carry messages between them. This idea was much elaborated in later Platonism, for example by Plutarch (AD

$50 - c$. 120) and Apuleius (second century AD). There is clearly a great deal in common between the idea of angels and that of daemons, and indeed Philo tells us that 'it is the custom of Moses [i.e., the custom of Scripture] to give the name of angels to those whom other philosophers call daemons'.[3] The idea of intermediary beings was still further elaborated in Neoplatonism, and as hierarchies of intermediary beings were developed, so the names for these beings were drawn from the Judaeo-Christian tradition, the Greek philosophical tradition, and other traditions too (such as Gnosticism). So, for instance, in his work *On the Mysteries of Egypt* the Neoplatonist Iamblichus has (usually) four ranks of beings mediating between the gods and human souls: archangels, angels, daemons, and heroes; he also refers to them by the term beloved of the Gnostics, *archons* (rulers).[4] In Christian use there developed a tendency to distinguish between angels and daemons, seeing in the angels *good* intermediary beings and in the daemons *evil* intermediaries (our 'demons'). This tendency was doubtless encouraged by the Christians' habit of regarding pagan gods as evil spirits who sought to deceive mankind. As the pagan philosophers interpreted their gods (or their presence amongst humans) as daemons, this led Christians to regard daemons as evil. In the stories of the early monks, the Desert Fathers of the fourth century, the demons are malevolent spiritual beings who tempt men to sin and faithlessness to Christ. Denys inherits this distinction: for him demons (*daimones*) are evil beings (evil not by nature, but through their freewill), though he has not very much to say about them (he mentions them, for example, in DN IV.23), while the angelic beings are those heavenly beings who have remained steadfast in their love of God.

THE ORDERING OF THE ANGELS ACCORDING TO DENYS

So much by way of background. We have mentioned that the Bible gives various names to these angelic beings: seraphim and cherubim, for instance. In the New Testament other names are given to such heavenly beings, notably by St Paul in Colossians 1:16 and Ephesians 1:21: there we read of thrones, dominions, principalities, authorities and powers. These—together with angel and archangel (the latter not found in the Old Testament, though it occurs in intertestamental literature and twice in the New Testament: 1 Thess 4:16 and Jude 9)—give the nine names of the angelic beings as we find them in Denys.

3 orders of 3

In Denys they appear as three ranks of three orders of beings: the first rank (in descending order), seraphim, cherubim, thrones; the second, dominions, powers, authorities; the third, principalities, archangels, angels.[5] There is nothing original in Denys's giving such a list of nine ranks of angelic beings. Earlier Christian writers had already put together these nine biblical names into a list of heavenly beings. St Cyril of Jerusalem (*c.* 315–86) gives just such a list (with the same names as Denys, though with a different order) as he enumerates the heavenly beings with whom we join our praises in the solemn prayer at the Eucharist.[6] St John Chrysostom (*c.* 347–407) in his *Homilies on Genesis*[7] gives another list of nine angelic beings (with the same names as Cyril and Denys, though his order is different from them both).[8] In his *Homilies on the Incomprehensibility of God*, Chrysostom has a good deal to say about the angelic beings: again he speaks of the same nine kinds of beings as Denys does, but here the order he gives differs even more from that of Denys.[9] Another fourth-century writer, St Gregory of Nyssa (*c.* 320–*c.* 395), shows interest in the ranks of angels. In his *Homilies on the Song of Songs* he speaks of the ranks of the angels and names them: his names are much what we would expect (and if, indeed, his ministers (*leitourgoi*) cover angels and archangels, the same), but his order is yet another permutation. Gregory is, however, very interested in their *ranks* as such: he emphasizes (against Origen) that the ranks of the angels are secure, and were unaffected by the fall of man. Their ordered array fills men and women with wonder and astonishment, and that wonder serves to keep them close to the path of virtue.[10] Chrysostom, too, finds the ranks of the angels awesome. So, too, later did the German poet, Rilke:

> Who, when I cry, hears me from out of the orders
> Of the angels? . . .
>   For the Beautiful is nothing
> But the onset of the fearful, which we can just bear,
> And we are amazed, because it disdains
> To destroy us. Every angel is fearful.[11]

One wonders whether there is any reason behind the developing interest in angels in the fourth century, which Denys takes a step further. The three Fathers we have mentioned—Cyril of Jerusalem, John Chrysostom, Gregory of Nyssa—all stood firm against the threat of Arianism, the two latter developing a doctrine of the complete unknowability of God against the arguments of the extreme Arian, Eunomius (d. 394). For Chrysostom and Gregory the doctrine of the angels fits into their emphasis on God's ineffability: even the angels cannot come to know God completely. Even though they reach more deeply than men and women could ever hope into the mystery of God, this closeness to God is characterized by silence.[12] The same idea is found in the Syrian Father, Ephrem (also fourth century): for instance in one of his *Hymns on the Faith* (4.1): 'A thousand thousands stand, ten thousand ten thousands run: thousands and ten thousands are not able to search into the One: for all of them in silence stand to minister.' The angels, as it were, display the utter ineffability of God, and come from that silence in which God dwells to communicate with men and women. Whereas earlier Christian theology had thought in terms of the Word (or *Logos*) of God coming from the silence that God is and declaring it,[13] and had interpreted the theophanies of God in the Old Testament as manifestations of the Word of God, Denys sees angels coming from the silence that God is (cf. DN IV.2), just as by the fifth century Christian theology had come increasingly to interpret theophanies as the work of angels.[14] Angels shroud, as it were, the greatly enhanced incomprehensibility of God.[15]

Denys, however, takes this growing interest in angels a step further, and in doing so lays the foundations for later theology. For he does not simply enumerate the nine ranks of angels, he sees them as constituting three orders, each consisting of three ranks of heavenly beings. No Christian writer before Denys produces this doubly threefold pattern (Denys himself attributes the idea to Hierotheus: CH VI.2). Where, we might wonder, does it come from? A Neoplatonic interest in triads is doubtless in the background. Proclus tells us that Iamblichus had 'three triads of intelligible gods'[16] in the 'intelligible hebdomad', which is very close to Denys's three triads of angels (who are also intelligible beings, that is, belonging to the realm of intellect or *nous*), and even earlier Porphyry (whose disciple Iamblichus had probably been) comments on one of the Chaldaean hymns (or oracles): 'This oracle gives knowledge of the three orders of angels: those who perpetually stand before God; those who are separated from him and who are sent forth with a view to certain messages and ministrations; those who perpetually bear his throne . . . and perpetually sing.'[17] So it looks as if Denys's distinctive contribution to Christian angelology is of Neoplatonic inspiration.

37

THE NOTION OF HIERARCHY

Three ranks of three, or three *hierarchies*, of angelic beings. Denys uses various words for the ranks or orders, but one of them, hierarchy (Greek: *hierarchia*) is first found in Denys himself and seems to be his own coinage. *Hierarch* (Greek: *hierarchēs*), the word he habitually uses for a bishop, is a pagan word meaning 'president of sacred rites, high-priest'.[18] But the word *hierarchia* is composed of two Greek words meaning 'sacred' and 'source or principle', and Denys probably expected his readers to be sensitive to etymology. He is fond, anyway, of coining words with the ending *-archia*. His normal word for the Godhead is Thearchy (*thearchia*); he uses words like *agatharchia* (from 'good' and 'source'), *taxiarchia* (from 'rank' and 'source'), and derives adjectives and verbs from the nouns thus arrived at: there is a verb, *hierarchein*, which presumably means 'to carry out the function of hierarchy'.

Hierarchy is a key term (and key concept) for Denys. He defines it several times. At the beginning of CH III, he introduces the term thus:

> Hierarchy is, as I understand it, a sacred order, knowledge and activity, which is being assimilated to likeness with God as much as possible and, in response to the illuminations that are given it from God, is raised to the imitation of Him in its own measure.

So hierarchy is more than just a rank or order; it refers as well to what this sacred ordering makes possible: knowledge and activity. The sacred order imparts knowledge and enables the members of the hierarchy to operate effectively. And the whole point of this sacred arrangement is an assimilation to the divine likeness. The purpose of hierarchy, its scope (*skopos*) as he puts it a few lines later, is assimilation to God and union with him, as far as possible. The whole arrangement is concerned with deification. 'Deification' is often thought of as clear evidence of the influence of Hellenistic ideas on Christian theology, but in fact the language which the Fathers use for deification (*theōsis, theopoiēsis*) is peculiar to the Christian tradition (the pagans speak, rather, of *apotheōsis*), and by the time of Denys it was firmly established in Christian vocabulary (especially in the Greek-speaking, and also the Syriac-speaking, traditions).[19]

It should therefore come as no surprise to find the language of deification so frequently used in the Dionysian writings. But what does it mean? Not some metaphysical confusion between God and his creatures: on the contrary, as we shall see, Denys holds quite firmly that creatures are created by God and have no ontological continuity with him. Rather, Denys means that creatures come to know God, and as 'like is known by like' (a maxim traditional in Greek philosophy), such knowledge implies a deepening likeness to God. Further, deification means for Denys that the deified creature becomes so united to God that its activity is the divine activity flowing through it. So, as he puts it, 'What could be more divine than to become, in the words of the oracles, a "fellow-worker with God" (1 Cor 3:9), and to show forth the divine energy which is manifested in oneself as much as one can?' (CH III.2).

Hierarchies mediate knowledge ('are knowledge', Denys actually says): they are vehicles of revelation. Denys conceives of this revelation in terms of light; light flowing out from the supreme Godhead and irradiating the whole created order. But it is not a light that shines *on* the created order, but rather *through* it: those nearest to God are illuminated and their brightness, derived ultimately from the brightness of God's glory, radiates the divine light further and further into the farthest recesses of the created order. The divine light is first of all received by the immaterial order of purely intellectual beings, the ranks of angels, arranged, as we have seen, three by three. From this purely intellectual level, the divine light is passed on to the material world, to men and women composed of souls and bodies, and in that realm it is the Church and its rites and ceremonies that are the vehicle of illumination. So Denys goes on, in CH III, to say,

> It is God himself who is our guide in all sacred knowledge and activity, and looking unwaveringly to his divine comeliness, the hierarchy receives his stamp as much as possible and makes its own members divine images, perfectly clear and spotless mirrors, receptive to the ray of the primordial and thearchic light, and divinely filled with the brilliance that has been given to it; and those in their turn, without envy, become sources of illumination for others, in accordance with the thearchic arrangements.

The hierarchies are a vehicle for theophany: they *are* a theophany. The divine light radiates out from the Godhead and reaches throughout the created order. And where the divine light shines, there God is. But the imagery of a light shining, though strongly biblical (cf. John 1:5), is also somewhat impersonal. Such impersonality is not, however, part of Denys's meaning. The last quotation makes clear

39

how much the passing on of the divine light depends on those who receive it, on their attentiveness and unwavering steadfastness. The light does not just shine, it is received and passed on. This sense of hierarchy as an active transmitter of the divine light is enormously important, and Denys expounds it by a triad that leaves its impress on almost every page of the works on the hierarchies. That is the triad of purification, illumination, and union or perfection (*katharsis, phōtismos, henōsis* or *teleiōsis*).

PURIFICATION, ILLUMINATION, UNION

The triad of purification, illumination and union is also something original to Denys that was destined to have a great impact on subsequent Christian tradition (the so-called 'three ways' of mysticism—the purgative way, the illuminative way, and the unitive way—are derived from it). Its origins can be sought partly in traditions associated with the pagan mystery religions: they required ritual purification as a preparation for initiation, and illumination and union could be said to be the fruit of such initiation. Plato picks up such language and uses it to give solemnity to his requirement of purification as preparation for the philosophical quest which, by means of illumination, finally achieves union with the objects of true knowledge. Christians too, had developed threefold patterns of ascent to God: Clement of Alexandria has an ethical stage, a 'hierurgical' stage which is said to be that of 'natural contemplation', and a final 'theological' stage, which is that of vision (or *epopteia*).[20] Similar triadic patterns can be found in Origen, Gregory of Nyssa, and Evagrius.[21] All these form the background for Denys's triad of purification, illumination, and union or perfection.

According to Denys, however, it is the triadic structure of the hierarchies that administer this threefold movement that purifies, illumines, and leads to union. In each triadic rank, the lowest order is purificatory or stands in need of purification; the middle order illumines or stands in need of illumination; the highest order leads to perfection or is led to perfection. The point of this seems threefold. First of all, the movement to union with God has three moments: purification is the foundation; this leads to illumination; which itself culminates in union or perfection. Secondly, purification, illumination and union are operations that happen to us: we *are* purified, we *are* illuminated, we *are* perfected. We do not achieve this movement

40

towards God ourselves, by our own efforts: we depend on God's gracious movement towards us. Denys's understanding of hierarchy is an expression of his deep sense of God's active search for mankind and gentle persuasion of fallen men. So in his letter to the monk Demophilus, he begs him to contemplate Christ:

> Let us quietly receive the beneficent rays of the truly good, the transcendently good Christ and let us be led by their light towards his divinely good deeds. After all is it not characteristic of his unspeakable, incomprehensible goodness that he fashions the existence of things, that he draws everything into being, that he wishes everything to be always akin to him and to have fellowship with him according to their fitness? Does he not come lovingly to those who have turned away from him? Does he not contend with them and beg them not to spurn his love? Does he not support his accusers and plead on their behalf? He even promises to be concerned for them and when they are far away from him they have only to turn back and there he is, hastening to meet them. He receives them with completely open arms and greets them with the kiss of peace. (Ep. VIII: 1085C–1088A)

Hierarchy is the outreach of God's love, it is not a ladder we struggle up by our own efforts. But thirdly, to depend on God and his love means to depend on other people. It is the members of the hierarchy who purify, illumine, and perfect, and themselves stand in need of such purification, illumination and perfection. The hierarchy is a community that is being saved and mediates salvation. Denys is often accused of a narrow individualism, because he seems concerned to show how the hierarchical arrangements meet the needs of the individual. But it is not so often noted that the hierarchical arrangements themselves are emphatically not impersonal, but are the arrangement of a community, or group of communities, whose members are seeking to draw near to God and draw others near to God. So Denys says:

> Since the order of hierarchy will mean that some are being purified and others purify, some are being enlightened while others enlighten, some are being perfected while others complete the perfecting initiation for others, each will imitate God in the way that is harmonious with its own functions. (CH III.2)

But what is mediated through this mutual assistance in the way to God comes from God himself, so Denys continues:

41

The Divine Blessedness, to speak in human terms, is free from any unlikeness, full of eternal light, perfect and lacking no perfection, itself purifying and enlightening and perfecting, or rather purification itself, illumination itself and perfection itself, the primary source and principle by itself of all perfecting initiation, beyond purification, beyond light, the source of all hierarchy, and yet separated by its transcendence from everything that is sacred.

HIERARCHY AND ORDER

Nonetheless, for many the very notion of order and hierarchy seems constraining: people are allotted their role and are to be content with it. In favour of the notion of hierarchy it could be argued that the alternative to some order is no order, and that anarchy brings with it much greater evils, much greater constraints on freedom and fulfilment. But Denys himself has none of these doubts or questions. He is deeply committed to the notion of an ordered society and sees the order he describes in the two books on the hierarchies as divinely ordained. He regards the principle of hierarchy as very precious. In Ep. VIII to the monk Demophilus who has broken the order of the hierarchy by rebuking a priest of whose ministrations he disapproved (and indeed driving him from the sanctuary), he asserts without qualification the principle of hierarchical order. Or perhaps not quite without any qualification: he insists that those who bear hierarchical office must be worthy of that office—an unworthy priest is no priest. But it is only one set over such a one hierarchically who can rebuke him. Further, Demophilus's offence was not just against hierarchical order, but against the whole purpose of hierarchy, which, as we have seen, is to express God's love and draw men and women to him: Demophilus had driven out of the sanctuary a priest who was reconciling a sinner.

But the assertion of hierarchical order in Ep. VIII is directly concerned with earthly hierarchy, which is not directly our concern in this chapter. In the *Celestial Hierarchy* itself there is an assertion of hierarchical order which might seem excessive (it has certainly seemed so to some). Although Jesus (that is, for Denys, the *incarnate* Son of God) is said to be the 'source and perfection of all hierarchies' (EH I.2), it is made quite clear that during his earthly life, Jesus was subject to angelic ministrations and like us had no direct, unmediated communion with God. In CH IV Denys argues that all human knowledge of divine things is mediated by angels, even the knowledge of Jesus' 'love of humanity', his *philanthrōpia* (as Denys habitually refers to the incarnation), was mediated by angels. And so in the case of the Incarnate Lord himself: 'Jesus himself, the transcendent Cause of those beings which live beyond the world, came to take on human form without in any way changing his own essential nature' and yet during his earthly life he 'submitted to the wishes of God the Father as arranged by angels'. There could hardly be any stronger assertion of Denys's respect for the principle of hierarchical order.

TALKING OF ANGELS

The *Celestial Hierarchy* is not just about the principle of hierarchy: it contains chapters on each of the three ranks of angelic beings and various other chapters on specific scriptural accounts of such angelic beings (for example, Isaiah's vision in the Temple and his being purified by one of the seraphim). Denys, then, has something to tell us about the angelic beings. What?

It might be better to ask, Why? Denys is not interested in clearing up some obscure points of celestial geography (if one can use such an expression) for their own sake. It is impossible for us to know 'the mysteries of the intelligences beyond the heavens', we can only know what God has revealed to us (CH III.1). And as the purpose of God's revelation is to draw mankind back to union with himself, the language of revelation is not there to convey information, but to raise us up to God. Revelation does not so much reveal something, as effect something.

In CH II Denys discusses the use of language in such revelation. Revelation concerning heavenly beings (and even more revelation of the Divine itself) makes use of language that refers to things within our earthly experience in order to draw us up to communion with that of which it speaks. Such language is symbolic. What is conveyed is not conveyed directly. To understand such language is to respond to it rightly; it is to be raised up towards the heavenly realm and thence to God. If we attempted to understand what the Scriptures say about heavenly beings simply and descriptively, then it would lead us into absurdity:

> One would likely then imagine that the heavens beyond really are filled with bands of lions and horses, that the divine praises are, in effect, great moos, that flocks of birds take wing there

43

or that there are other kinds of creatures all about or even more dishonourable material things. (CH II.2)

Denys gives two reasons for 'creating types for the typeless, for giving shape to what is actually without shape':

First, we lack the ability to be directly raised up to conceptual contemplations. We need our own upliftings that come naturally to us and which can raise before us the permitted forms of the marvellous and unformed sights. Secondly, it is most fitting to the mysterious passages of scripture that the sacred and hidden truth about the celestial intelligences be concealed through the inexpressible and the sacred and be inaccessible to the many. Not everyone is sacred, and, as scripture says, knowledge is not for everyone. (CH II.2)

This latter point, that the obscurity of the Scriptures is intended to protect their secrets from the profane, we have already come across in St Basil (see above, p. 27), and it is common in the Fathers. St Augustine saw such obscurity as a challenge to our pride, since it demands of the reader a humble, patient effort to understand.[22] The modern Orthodox theologian, Vladimir Lossky, spoke of a 'margin of silence' belonging to the words of Scripture, 'which cannot be picked up by the ears of those outside'.[23] Only those who can discern this margin of silence are able to enter into the real meaning of the Scriptures. It is only in a spirit of prayer that we can become attuned to this silence. But the first reason Denys gives for the use of symbolic, and apparently absurd, language in Scripture is that we are incapable, as beings of flesh and blood caught up in the concerns of the material world, of being lifted up by 'conceptual contemplations', that is, by immaterial representations of angelic matters. They would simply pass us by, we would miss the point. Part of Denys's point here is a point that is commonplace amongst Platonists. It is by abstraction that we form immaterial concepts, by thinking away the particular and the material, but whereas properly such abstraction should lead us to a deeper grasp of reality, it can often go the other way; by thinking away the particular and material we simply drain our thoughts of any grasp on reality at all. So abstraction, the formation of immaterial concepts, is not a simple operation, but an exercise, a practice, by which the human mind is weaned from its dependence on the material and particular and accustomed to the more austere world of pure, immaterial truth. Plato (and the Neoplatonists were with him in this) thought that mathematics was indispensable for the soul in its transition from the material to the conceptual. That gave the whole ascent to the divine a strongly intellectual bias which Christians tended to resist; mathematics was, consequently, much less important in Christian circles.

LIKE AND UNLIKE SYMBOLISM

The symbolic language of Scripture, then, at once conceals the inner meaning from the eyes of the merely curious and provides images that are within our grasp and can be of use in our ascent to God. Within this symbolic language Denys distinguishes between like and unlike symbols (*homoia* and *anomoia symbola*). Some symbols have some similarity to that which they symbolize: Denys gives the examples of reason, mind and being. When Scripture describes God in these terms, it depicts God as rational, intelligent, a supreme Being to whom all other beings owe their existence. Other symbols are drawn from the material world and many of them seem ridiculous: Denys does not give any examples in this chapter of the *Celestial Hierarchy*, but in Ep. IX he gives a long list of such apparently inappropriate symbolism and concentrates particularly on extreme anthropomorphisms—God as a man of war, or a passionate lover, or as jealous, deceitful, or arrayed in tasteless jewellery.

But Denys insists that it is this unlike symbolism that is more appropriate to God, because in fact God infinitely transcends anything we say about him. If we depict him using like symbolism and see him as, for example, an omnipotent, far-seeing creator, we are very likely to make the mistake of supposing that God is really like that: a being among other beings, only much more powerful and indeed the one to whom all other beings owe their existence. But that is not so, God is not a being among other beings, even a very powerful one: he utterly transcends every being and any conception we may have of him. If, however, we use unlike symbolism of God, and say that he is a man of war or a consuming fire, then there is little danger we will imagine that he is really like that. It will be obvious that such language tells us something about God, but does not describe him.

The truest kind of language about God, according to Denys, is that which *denies* qualities of God, as when we say that he is invisible, infinite, ineffable. Such a way of negation describes God truly,

45

since God is in no way like the things that have being. Since unlike symbolism compels us to seek understanding of God by denying what we say about him, it is more reliable. As Denys puts it, 'Since the way of negation appears to be more suitable to the realm of the divine and since positive affirmations are always unfitting to the hiddenness of the inexpressible, a manifestation through dissimilar shapes is more correctly applied to the invisible' (CH II.3).

This applies, too, to the invisible realm of the angels. Scripture deliberately describes the heavenly beings as horses, cows, wheels and so forth, for there is less danger we will understand such language literally. If Scripture had used what is nearest to the angelic realm to describe it (the human realm) we might easily depict the angels as simply superhuman—'golden and gleaming men, glamorous, wearing lustrous clothing', as Denys puts it (and how right he was!); whereas 'the sheer crassness of the signs is a goad so that even the materially inclined cannot accept that it could be permitted or true that the celestial and divine sights could be conveyed by such shameful things'. Such language, Denys adds, also reminds us that 'there is nothing which lacks its own share of beauty, for as Scripture rightly says, "Everything is good" '. 'A goad': that is the point of such language, not to describe but to stir up our devotion and lift us up towards heaven.

Denys goes on to apply these principles to the way in which human emotions are applied to the transcendent realm. It is worth pausing to consider this, for there were two currents in Christian ascetic literature contemporary with Denys. All (or nearly all) saw the attainment of *apatheia* (freedom from passions or emotions) as the goal of Christian ascetic struggle: such freedom from passions was seen as releasing a pure love for God and for men. Some saw *apatheia* as suppression of the passions: that was the tendency of the Evagrian tradition;[24] others saw *apatheia* as a transformation of the passions, a redirection of them: Diadochus, Theodoret (both fifth century) and later Maximus the Confessor (*c*. 580–662) are representatives of such a tradition. Denys's interpretation of the way human emotions are applied to the celestial realm suggests that he belonged to the second tradition: for if such feelings have meaning in the transcendent realm, that sublimation is presumably the goal for our ascetic endeavour here below. So anger is interpreted as 'the sturdy working of reason in [the celestial beings] and the capacity they have to be grounded tenaciously in holy and unchanging foundations': the sublimation of anger is a kind of rational strength and sturdiness. Desire becomes 'a strong and sure desire for the clear and impassible contemplation of the transcendent. It is a hunger for an unending, conceptual, and true communion with the spotless and sublime light, of clear and splendid beauty.' Denys would have understood Diadochus, nearly his (older) contemporary, when he spoke of the 'fire of *apatheia*'.[25]

THE ORDERS OF ANGELS

Most of the *Celestial Hierarchy* is concerned with applying these principles to understanding what is said about angels in the Scriptures. He treats each rank separately and then looks at various particular problems. He has a good deal to say about the first hierarchy of angelic beings, the seraphim, cherubim, and thrones (CH VII). He gives the traditional meanings of the Hebrew names: seraphim means 'fire-makers', that is to say, 'carriers of warmth'; cherubim means 'fullness of knowledge' or 'outflowing of wisdom'. This rank of angelic beings is immediately present before God, his revelation is received by them first. Denys then goes on to expound this basic information, making use, as he does so, of Neoplatonic themes.

Thus the name seraphim means 'a perennial circling around the divine things, penetrating warmth, the overflowing heat of a movement which never falters and never fails, a capacity to stamp their own image on subordinates by arousing and uplifting in them too a like flame, a like warmth'; cherubim signify 'the power to know and see God, to receive the greatest gifts of his light, to contemplate the divine splendour in primordial power, to be filled with the gifts that bring wisdom and to share these generously with subordinates as a part of the beneficent outpouring of wisdom'; thrones suggest 'a transcendence over every earthly defect, as shown by their upward-bearing toward the ultimate heights, that they are forever separated from what is inferior . . . and are utterly available to receive the divine visitation, that they bear God and are ever open, like servants, to welcome God' (CH VII.1).

The leading motif behind this interpretation of the three highest beings is the triad purification – illumination – perfection: the thrones 'transcend defects', in this way representing purification; emphasis is laid on the contemplative power of the cherubim, corresponding to illumination; the seraphim represent perfection in their continual union with God. Denys goes on to draw out the significance of this at some length (VII.2). His discussion is something of a *tour de force*, as the natural meaning of purification (which is

47

mainly a matter of turning from sin) and illumination (in the sense of filling a need) is inappropriate in the exalted realm of the first hierarchy. But not entirely, at least in the realm of illumination; for even to the angelic hierarchies the incarnation is something new, something they have to learn about. Psalm 24:10, with its question 'Who is the King of Glory?' celebrates the angelic questioning as Jesus ascends into heaven in human form: the Lord of hosts, the Lord of the heavenly powers, he is the King of Glory, is their answer.

> Others, as they puzzle over the nature of Jesus, acquire an understanding of this divine work on our behalf and it is Jesus himself who is their instructor, teaching them directly about the kindly work he has undertaken out of love for man. 'I speak of righteousness and saving judgement.' (VII.3)

The last scriptural quotation, placed on the lips of Jesus, is from Isaiah 63:1 (in the form found in the Greek Bible, the Septuagint), and is the answer to the question, 'Who is this that comes from Edom, in crimsoned garments from Bozrah, he that is marching in his apparel, marching in the greatness of his strength?'. The answer provokes another question, 'Why is thy apparel red, and thy garments like his that treads in the wine press?', which leads into the splendid song of verses 3–6. The Fathers, from Origen onwards,[26] had interpreted this questioning as a questioning of Jesus by the angelic beings. But the first question is not directly addressed to Jesus, though he answers it, and Denys sees in this a marked similarity between those exalted beings and us when it comes to enlightenment in divine matters: 'They do not first ask, "Why are your garments red?". They begin by exchanging queries among themselves, thus showing their eagerness to learn and their desire to know how God operates. They do not simply go leaping beyond that outflow of enlightenment provided by God.' It is a splendid picture of the highest angelic beings wondering among themselves, as Christ re-enters heaven in his wounded humanity.

As the angels surround God and 'dance around an eternal knowledge of him' (VII.4), they celebrate their gloriously transcendent enlightenment with hymns of praise: 'Some of these hymns, if one may use perceptible images, are like the "sound of many waters" . . . others thunder out that famous and venerable song telling of God: "Holy, holy, holy is the Lord of hosts. The whole earth is full of his glory".'

Denys then goes on to discuss the second rank of angelic beings: dominions, powers, and authorities (CH VIII). Oddly, he does not seem very sure about the order of the heavenly beings in this intermediate rank: his normal order is what we have given, but once (the first time he mentions them, at CH VI.2: 201A) he interposes the dominions and powers; and once (at the beginning of VIII: 237B) he seems to interpose the powers and authorities. Not surprisingly, Denys uses this chapter on the intermediate rank of angels to say something about mediation, about the 'process of handing on from angel to angel' which is a 'symbol for us of the perfection which comes complete from afar and grows dimmer as it proceeds' (VIII.2).

The final hierarchy consists of principalities, archangels, and angels. This is the angelic hierarchy that directly presides over 'human hierarchies' (oddly in the plural: 260B) and the different nations are allotted to different angels, Israel's angelic ruler being Michael (whom Denys does not seem to regard as an archangel). The idea of guardian angels for nations is found in the Bible (e.g., Dan 10:13, 20f.), and the same belief is found among Neoplatonists, for instance in Iamblichus.[27] Denys explains the election of Israel, in contrast to the faithlessness to the truth of the pagan nations, in terms not of special divine favour, but of Israel's faithfulness that made them worthy of God's special favour. Unlike other nations, Israel did not desert its angelic illumination, and thus it merited being called God's people (CH IX.3).

The rest of the *Celestial Hierarchy* deals with various problems presented by the language that Scripture uses to describe the celestial beings. In particular, Denys is worried about apparent breaches of hierarchical order, such as when Isaiah is said to be visited by one of the seraphim, instead of by an angel. His long and involved attempt to answer this problem struggles both to maintain the principle of hierarchy and to preserve his conviction that what is mediated through the hierarchies is God's own activity: a point, he argues, which is made by attributing human purification in this case to one of the seraphim (CH XIII). Other breaches of hierarchy are seen in the application of the term 'angel' to angelic beings in general (easily solved in that the higher can be held to contain the lower: CH V), and in the way all such beings are sometimes called 'powers' (less easily solved, and more of a problem, perhaps, because it was something of an established tradition in Christian circles to refer to celestial beings as powers[28]). This latter is solved by the introduction of the Neoplatonic doctrine (derived ultimately from Aristotle's distinction between potentiality and actuality) that every mind possesses being, power and activity:[29] so just as we call the heavenly minds 'beings', we could equally well call them 'powers' (CH XI). The final chapter of the *Celestial Hierarchy* deals with the corporeal images used of the angels in detail.

So in the *Celestial Hierarchy* Denys introduces us to the principle of hierarchy that informs his understanding of the universe. The glorious array of the celestial realms manifests and passes on the effulgence of the divine glory. Just as the celestial hierarchy is an 'image of the thearchic comeliness' (165B), so the earthly hierarchy, among which we find our own place, mirrors at a still lower level the splendour of the celestial hierarchy. To that hierarchy, 'our' hierarchy, as Denys calls it, we shall now turn.

Notes

1   See MT III: 1033A – B; there are examples of symbolic theology in CH, e.g., at II.5.

2   On the subject of angels in the Fathers, see J. Daniélou, *Les Anges et leur mission* (Chevetogne, 1951), and, more generally (especially good for their iconography), P. L. Wilson, *Angels* (London, 1980). See also the new Blackfriars edition of St Thomas Aquinas, *Summa Theologiae*, vol. 9 (Ia, 50–64), by Kenelm Foster, OP (London, 1967).

3   Philo, *On the Giants* 6.

4   Iamblichus, *On the Mysteries* II.4 (78); cf. II.7 (83): ed. E. des Places (Paris, 1966), pp. 84f., 87f.

5   The Greek words for the angelic beings of the second and third ranks are: *kyriotēs, dynamis, exousia*; *archē, archangelos, angelos*. Note how the form of the words suggests *archangelos* as an intermediary between *archē* and *angelos*.

6   *Catechetical Lecture* 23 (5th Mystagogical), 6. (These homilies may be by Cyril's successor in the see of Jerusalem, John.)

7   John Chrysostom, *Homily on Genesis* 4.5.

8   See Roques, *Structures*, pp. 111ff.

9   See the introduction by J. Daniélou to the edition of Chrysostom's homilies *On the Incomprehensibility of God* in *Sources Chrétiennes* (28 bis; Paris, 1970), pp. 40–50.

10   Homily XV in *Gregorii Nysseni Opera* (ed. W. Jaeger), vol. VI, pp. 445f.

11   Rilke, *Duineser Elegien*, I, 11.1–2, 4–7.

12   See J. Daniélou, *op. cit.*, pp. 46f. and the passages cited there.

13   See Ignatius, *Epistle to the Magnesians* 8.2.

14   E.g. in the West, Augustine, *On the Trinity* III, and cf. CH IV.3.

15   See Koch, *Ps-Dionysius*, pp. 131f.

16   Proclus, *Commentary on the Timaeus*, ed. E. Diehl, vol. 1 (Leipzig, 1903), p. 308, 1.21.

17   Quoted in H. Lewy, *Chaldaean Oracles and Pagan Theurgy* (rev. ed., Paris, 1978), pp. 13f. (text: n. 31).

18   See Liddell and Scott, *Greek-English Lexicon*, s.v.

19   For the Syrian tradition, see Sebastian Brock, *The Luminous Eye* (Rome, 1985), pp. 123–8.

20   Clement of Alexandria, *Stromateis* I.28.176.1ff.

21   See my *Origins of the Christian Mystical Tradition* (Oxford, 1981), pp. 58–60 (for Origen), 84–7 (for Gregory), 102f. (for Evagrius).

22   See Augustine, *On Christian Doctrine* II.6.7f.

23   See Vladimir Lossky's essay, 'Tradition and Traditions' in *In the Image and Likeness of God* (Eng. trans., London and Oxford, 1974), p. 151.

24   *Origins of the Christian Mystical Tradition*, *op. cit.*, pp. 103–10.

25   Diadochus, *Gnostic Chapters* 17 (ed. E. des Places, *Sources Chrétiennes*, 5ter, Paris 1966: p. 94); though Denys himself only rarely uses the word *apatheia*: the passage just quoted contains one such use. 'Anger' and 'desire' in the passages just quoted (from CH II.4) represent the Greek words *thymos* and *epithymia*, the names for the two lower parts of the soul in Plato's analysis (*Republic* IV.434D–441C; cf. *Phaedrus* 246A–247C, *Timaeus* 69B–71D), which was widely accepted in the Christian ascetic tradition.

26   See Origen, *Commentary on John* VI.56. There is nothing strange in Denys's interpretation here, as Rorem's note seems to suggest (*Works*, p. 164, n. 78).

27   *On the Mysteries* V.25, and see note in *Sources Chrétiennes* ed. of CH (58 bis, Paris, 1970): p. 132, n. 1.

28   J. Daniélou, *op. cit.*, p. 40.

29   See Proclus, *Elements of Theology*, prop. 169, and E. R. Dodds's note in his edition (2nd ed., Oxford, 1963), p. 288.

4

The earthly liturgy

OUR HIERARCHY

Hierarchy, we have seen, is concerned with communicating the Divine Light from the source of that Light, God himself, and drawing all rational creatures back into union with the Supreme Beauty. In the hierarchy of the angelic beings we see this diaphanous manifestation of the divine glory, and the receiving and passing on of that glory, in pure conditions: conditions of pure, spiritual reality. Now in the *Ecclesiastical Hierarchy*, we see the extension of the outreach of God's alluring love into the human realm. These 'human hierarchies' (as Denys calls them: 260B) reflect the same principles as the angelic ones: they take the form of triads, the triads express the threefold movement of purification, illumination and perfection, and the purpose of the whole arrangement is to draw rational beings up to union with God and deify them. Things are different, though, with 'our hierarchy' (as Denys habitually refers to it: the expression 'ecclesiastical hierarchy' only occurs in the title of the work), mainly because whereas the angels are purely spiritual beings, men and women are composed of body and soul.

The difference this makes comes out very clearly in chapter V, at the beginning of his discussion of the ranks of the clergy. There he says that every hierarchy is divided into three. He specifies this triad as sacraments (*teletai*), those who understand the sacraments and initiate others into them (the clergy), and those who are initiated by them into the sacraments (what we would call the laity). There is nothing odd about the hierarchies' being structured in triads, but in the case of the angelic hierarchies, as we have seen, the members of the triads are all angelic beings; there is nothing corresponding to sacraments. To define hierarchy as a triad consisting of sacraments, initiators and initiates fits 'our' hierarchy, but is very awkward in relation to the celestial hierarchy, as transpires when Denys tries to show how this definition of hierarchy is exemplified in the case of the angelic beings (CH V.2).

He then suggests a way of looking at our hierarchy as midway between the celestial hierarchy and the hierarchy of the Old Testament, which he calls the 'hierarchy of the Law'.[1] In the hierarchy of the Law, truth was veiled with obscure imagery and only discerned with great difficulty behind dense enigmas. Such a heavy veil of symbolism was necessary to protect the weak eyes of the men of the Old Covenant. In the celestial hierarchy there is found the power of contemplative understanding. Our hierarchy is a mean between the two, where symbolism is used and contemplative understanding is attained.

Denys's analogy here does not work at all well. We know very well by now that there is no *direct* contemplation of God, even in the celestial hierarchy; nor could the symbolism in the Old Testament be *mere* symbolism, for unless it symbolized something it would not be symbolic at all. But nonetheless the point still holds, that our hierarchy partakes of both the material order and the spiritual order. It uses symbols from the material order and attains contemplation in the spiritual order. And such a middle position corresponds to our middle position as human beings, composed of both body and soul.

Our hierarchy, then, is a triad of sacraments, ministers and those to whom they minister. And each part of this triad again forms a triad: there are three sacraments, three orders of clergy, and three orders of laity. The three sacraments are the sacrament of illumination (baptism), the sacrament of gathering together (the Greek is *synaxis*: the sacrament is the Eucharist), and the sacrament of oil (*myron*). The three orders of clergy are hierarchs, priests, and ministers (*leitourgoi*): which we recognize as the threefold ministry of bishops, priests (usually called presbyters—literally, elders—in ecclesiastical language until long after Denys's time: 'presbyter' occurs in CA only in the dedications of the treatises, which may not be original) and deacons. The three orders of laity are monks, the 'sacred people' (what we would call the 'laity', from the Greek for 'people', *laos*, used here by Denys), and those who have yet to be initiated or who have spoilt their initiation and consequently been excluded from the sacred people. The latter group includes catechumens (those preparing for baptism), penitents (those guilty of grave sin, who have been excluded from communion for a period) and the possessed (that is, the mad, those possessed by demons and consequently driven away from rational communion with sacred things).

The significance of this hierarchical ordering can be understood in various ways. First of all, it corresponds to the triad of purification, illumination and perfection. The lowest order of those being initiated—the catechumens, penitents and the possessed—stand in need of purification and are being purified. The sacred people are being illuminated, and are consequently called the 'contemplative order'. The monks are being perfected. The deacons are responsible for the duty of purifying: they are entrusted with the task of giving instruction in the Scriptures and the faith to the catechumens (not all that earlier, this had been pre-eminently an episcopal task: all the 'Catechetical Homilies' of the fourth century are the work of bishops), and also with the liturgical duty of seeing that the catechumens and others are excluded from the church after the readings from the Scriptures. The priests' task is to illuminate: thus their concern is especially with the sacred people. The hierarch's (or bishop's) task is to perfect, and the monks, therefore, are their especial concern. It will be seen that the triad of ministers and the triad of those ministered to relates very straightforwardly to the triad of purification, illumination and perfection. This is not so with the sacraments, however: baptism is called 'illumination', though it is purifying as well, and the Eucharist and the sacrament of oil are both said to be perfecting.

A further significance of this hierarchical ordering might be called geographical. In his letter to Demophilus (Ep. VIII) Denys gives an account of the ordering of the different ranks in the church building, an account we can supplement from various descriptions of the rites in EH. The church of Denys's day was clearly already divided inside, with a sanctuary separated off from the main body of the church by the 'holy doors' (as they are still called today in the Orthodox Church): it is even possible that this separation was made by a screen covered with splendidly painted symbols (perhaps icons, as on the iconostasis of a modern Orthodox church: EH III.iii.2: 428C). The three orders of ministers were allowed inside this sanctuary; the laity were kept outside. Amongst the laity, the monks had a special place close to the holy doors of the sanctuary, though Denys emphasizes that they are not placed there 'like sentries', rather their being placed outside the holy doors indicates that they are closer to the people than to the priests. The catechumens, penitents and possessed are allowed into the church building for the first part of the liturgy, but are excluded from the celebration of the Eucharist and Communion. All this gives us a clear picture of the Christian community assembled for worship, a picture that corresponds well with what we know from other sources, for instance the *Homilies on Baptism and the Eucharist* of Theodore of Mopsuestia, where we have a picture of worship in the Church of West Syria at the beginning of the fifth century.[2] The ordered arrangement of the church fits well with Denys's hierarchical idea in general and, more especially, reflects his idea of graded participation in the divine mysteries, with a secret source at the centre, veiled from the outer reaches.

One point, though, is striking, and that is that it is a very masculine picture. Presumably the laity included women as well as men, and there might have been women amongst the ranks of the monks. But there is not a word of it. And it *is* surprising, for in the church of Denys's day (and especially in the church in Syria) women played a varied role. The *Didascalia*, which gives a picture of the life of the church in Syria in the late third century, has a good deal to say about the order of widows, whose special duty was prayer. An order of deaconesses is mentioned there, too. In the rite of baptism throughout the Church, deaconesses had a special role to play in the triple immersion in the case of women: but Denys represents this task as being fulfilled not by deacons but by the hierarch himself. Widows, deaconesses and virgins had an important part in the Church of the fourth century, and seem to have had a special place reserved for them in the church building.[3] But we hear nothing of this in Denys. Such a position for women did eventually die out, or become reserved for those living a specifically conventual life, but it does not seem that this had happened by the time of Denys. Councils in the East in the sixth century were exercised about deaconesses arrogating to themselves too much: so they must have been important enough to be a nuisance!

THE *ECCLESIASTICAL HIERARCHY*[4]

The structure of the *Ecclesiastical Hierarchy* is both more and less formalized than that of the *Celestial Hierarchy*: more, in that it does not have chapters on particular problems, but less, in that its structure is not very clearly related to the triads that constitute 'our' hierarchy. The first chapter is introductory. The next three chapters discuss the three rites or sacraments. Chapter V discusses the clergy and revolves round an account of the service of ordination. Chapter VI discusses the lay orders and concentrates on the service of monastic consecration. Chapter VII is concerned with the funeral service. After the first chapter, each of the chapters is divided into three: first an introductory section, then a section called the 'mystery' (*mystērion*), and finally a section called 'contemplation' (*theōria*). The second section is always an account of a rite or ceremony; the third section is an interpretation of it, an interpretation by which we enter into the significance of what is symbolized in the rite and thus raised up towards God.

The symbolic rites have been handed down in an unwritten tradition: in this Denys concurs with the teaching of St Basil that we are already familiar with (see above, pp. 26–27). They are thus 'more immaterial' and in a way superior to the Scriptures (EH I.4). As the Scriptures preserve their inner meaning from the gaze of the curious by means of the obscurity of their symbolism (above, p. 44), so the sacramental rites of the Church preserve their inner meaning by being protected by the *disciplina arcani*, a discipline of secrecy, whereby only baptized members of the Church are admitted to the sacraments and all others excluded. This is possibly the explanation of what is, at first sight, a contradiction in Denys: that he extols 'unlike symbolism' when expounding scriptural imagery for the angels or God, but in his accounts of the sacraments, he often stresses the appropriateness of the symbolism and of the symbolic value of the material elements used. 'Unlike symbolism' is its own protection; the sacraments are already protected, by the *disciplina arcani*. This *disciplina arcani* was certainly adhered to in the fourth century (and so written versions of homilies on the sacraments do not disclose the actual words of the sacramental rites), but it declined as infant baptism became more and more the norm and so any distinction between the Church and the society amongst which it lived was eroded. How far this process had gone by the time of Denys we do not know: but the form of the liturgy still assumed its existence, and still does in the Orthodox churches (the deacon still calls out for the doors to be closed at the time when the catechumens were excluded: as early as the seventh century the meaning of this exclamation had been lost—Maximus the Confessor gives an edifying allegorization[5]). Denys assumes the *disciplina arcani* as a fact, and goes to the length of producing a tortuous Greek periphrasis to avoid mentioning the Hebrew word, 'alleluia', and thus setting it down in writing.[6]

The bare account of the sacramental rite (the 'mystery') is expounded in the much longer 'contemplation' (*theōria*). The use of *theōria* here parallels earlier exegetical practice: it is the normal word for the deeper meaning of Scripture among the Antiochene exegetes (for example John Chrysostom and Theodore of Mopsuestia), and is also found in this sense in Gregory of Nyssa. Denys transfers it from biblical exegesis to sacramental interpretation. The rites and ceremonies of the Church are a moving outwards, into the multiplicity of spatial form and temporal succession, that is to be met by our participation and understanding which will accomplish our elevation towards God, our union with him, and our deification: the end and purpose of hierarchy. As Rorem notes, the threefold pattern of these chapters corresponds to the movement of procession and return, characteristic of Neoplatonism.[7]

THE SACRAMENTS

As we have seen, Denys enumerates three sacramental rites (*teletai*)—baptism, the Eucharist, and the sacrament of oil—and also expounds three other services—ordination, monastic consecration, and the funeral service. This list, taken either way, does not bear much relation to the list of seven sacraments, taken as traditional in the West. That is hardly surprising, as the list of seven sacraments—baptism, confirmation, the Eucharist, marriage, ordination, penance, and the anointing of the sick (or extreme unction)—does not emerge until the twelfth century, though it then won rapid acceptance in the West. In the East, however, the list of seven sacraments only became common much later, as a result of Western influence, and it is not surprising that lists of sacraments among the Orthodox, rarely thought of as definitive, are often reminiscent of Denys. Theodore the Studite, in the ninth century, gives a list of six sacraments—the holy 'illumination' (baptism), the 'synaxis' (the Eucharist), the holy chrism, ordination, monastic tonsure, and the service of burial[8]—while Nicolas Cabasilas's book *The Life in Christ* is a commentary on baptism, chrismation and the Eucharist.[9] There seems to be a certain difference of feel between the Western list and those inspired by Denys: the latter are seen very much as ecclesiastical rites, whereas the former is a series of significant events in the life of the individual Christian. Denys himself, however, only calls baptism, the Eucharist, and the sacrament of oil sacraments or rites (*teletai*): the other three ceremonies are not enumerated with them. It is probably not even correct to think of the three rites as 'sacraments', in anything like our sense of the word: the sacrament of oil, at least, does not correspond to any single 'sacrament' (such as confirmation or chrismation). Denys describes the *blessing* of the oil: its use seems to be various—he mentions the anointings in the course of baptism and the use of oil in the consecration of the altar.

BAPTISM

The first of the rites, properly so called, is baptism, which Denys always calls by one of its traditional names, 'illumination' (*phōtisma*, so called by Clement of Alexandria, Gregory of Nyssa and others): the word 'baptism' is only used twice and refers not to the whole ceremony but to the immersion in water (the word, *baptisma*, means dipping). The New Testament has two main ways of understanding baptism: as rebirth (especially characteristic of the Johannine tradition), and as death and resurrection (especially characteristic of St Paul). Denys, though he does not ignore the Pauline tradition (immersion, *baptisma*, symbolizes our sharing in Christ's death: EH II.iii.6: 404A), primarily sees baptism as rebirth, thus following the Johannine tradition, which had also been characteristic of early Syriac Christianity as a whole.[10] This rebirth is a divine birth (*theogenesia*) which makes possible deification. Denys refers to the teaching of Hierotheus that 'in the realm of intellect it is the love of God which first of all moves us towards the divine': in baptism, it is the love of God that gives us a divine beginning, a divine birth, and enables us to move towards the divine.

Denys then moves on to the second section, the mystery, and gives an account of the baptismal rite. It begins when someone 'fired by love of transcendent reality and longing for a sacred share of it' seeks out a Christian, who takes him to the bishop. The bishop rejoices, like the shepherd who found the lost sheep, and calling together the clergy marks him with the sign of the cross and has him enrolled as a catechumen. Then a description of the baptismal rite follows: the stripping and renunciation of Satan (facing West), followed by the candidate's turning East and confessing Christ, the pre-baptismal anointing, the blessing of the water of baptism (into which oil is poured), the triple immersion, the clothing, post-baptismal anointing and signing with the cross, and then participation in the celebration of the Eucharist.[11] The 'contemplation' which completes the chapter dwells on the significance of these ceremonies. What is strikingly missing from Denys's interpretation here is any real sensitivity to what one might call the 'typological' significance of baptism. Traditional Christian interpretation of the sacraments saw the symbolic actions as echoing Old Testament types of God's activity. The use of water recalled events such as the crossing of the Red Sea by the Israelites, and the Flood in which the sinners were destroyed and Noah and his family saved in the ark (cf. 1 Pet 3:18–21). Admittedly, Denys keeps the most fundamental typological significance of baptism, that in it we share in the death of Christ, but he has scarcely any reference to the Old Testament types by which Christians had, for centuries, drawn out the significance of baptism. The events of the baptismal rite are material symbols of immaterial truth, and the main truth, at this stage, is the reverence in which we should hold the sacred hierarchical arrangements.

'An image of this harmonious and sacred order is the reverence of the postulant, his self-awareness, the path he takes, with the help of his sponsor, towards the hierarch' (EH II.iii.4: 400C). The renunciation facing West and the turning East to confess Christ symbolize the utter opposition between the life the postulant is renouncing and the one he is seeking: and this opposition is expressed in terms of the dividedness of a life of wickedness and the unity of a life in pursuit of the One. The anointings are symbols of the strength and resoluteness that will be needed to persevere: they are anointings, like that of a wrestler, for the struggle to which the Christian is committed by his baptism. The immersion symbolizes, as we have seen, our sharing in Christ's death: death, Denys makes a point of saying, is 'the separation of two parts which had been linked together. It brings the soul into what for us is an invisible realm where it, in the loss of the body, becomes formless' (404B). This formlessness is interpreted as a kind of receptiveness to the illumination that is the heart of this rite. It is symbolized by the bright clothes put on: 'His courage and his likeness to God, his firm thrust towards the One, make him indifferent to all contrary things. Order descends upon disorder within him. Form takes over from formlessness. Light shines through all his life' (404C). The final anointing and the fragrance it brings symbolizes the anointing with the Holy Spirit and its ineffability. René Roques wonders if we do not find in this chapter a deliberate substitution of the Platonic contrast sensible–intelligible (*aisthētos–noēton*) for the traditional, Christian contrast type–truth.[12] It is hard not to feel that he is right. And the idea of symbols as pointing away from the material towards the spiritual is underlined by Denys's further tendency, which we have noticed, to gloss this as a move from dividedness/multiplicity to unity/the One.

THE EUCHARIST

The movement from the One to multiplicity and back again governs Denys's understanding of the Eucharist. He calls it, we have seen, the *synaxis*, the 'gathering-together' of the many into unity. It is, for Denys, the most important of the sacraments: he says that his 'celebrated teacher', Hierotheus, had called it the 'rite of rites', or 'sacrament of sacraments' (*teletōn teletē*), and as he expounds this he plays on the associations of the word *teletē*, which recalls *telos*, end or purpose, and *teleiōsis*, perfection. No other rite can take place without the Eucharist, so that they are only perfected by its means. And each 'sacredly initiating operation', thus perfected by the Eucharist, 'draws our fragmented lives together into a one-like deification. It forges a divine unity out of the divisions within us. It grants us communion and union with the One.'

Denys's account of the celebration of the Eucharist has many points in common with that given by Theodore of Mopsuestia in his Homilies on the Eucharist, which is not surprising if Denys is recording the liturgical customs of some part of Syria. There is an initial censing. The first part of the liturgy consists of psalm singing and readings from the Scriptures (by the deacons), and then the catechumens, penitents and possessed leave (supervised by the deacons). The Creed is sung (something not found in Theodore's rite: as we have seen, it was only introduced towards the end of the fifth century), the kiss of peace follows and then there takes place the intercession for the living and (especially) the departed, during which the deacons and priests place the bread and wine on the altar. Then follows the Eucharistic Prayer, communion, and a final prayer of thanksgiving.

But Denys's account is selective. He is primarily concerned with the *movement* of the liturgical action, and sees that movement almost exclusively in terms of God's love outwards to us in creation and redemption, drawing us back to him in our own answering movement of love. It is the Neoplatonic movement of procession and return that is most prominent. In contrast, Theodore is concerned with much more of the liturgical action and relates it much more directly to the historical events of Christ's life that are recalled in the liturgy. So for Theodore the first part of the liturgy, the readings, is concerned with the prophecies of Christ's life and that life and ministry itself; and the sacramental liturgy is modelled on the laying of the dead body of Jesus in the tomb and its being wrapped in linen clothes (so Theodore refers to the deacons' laying the linen on the altar, something Denys ignores) and the resurrection through the life-giving power of the Spirit which is echoed in the invocation of the Spirit (the epiclesis) in the consecratory prayer. Theodore also tells us about the movement of the deacons to and fro between the sanctuary and the nave, where the people are: a movement he compares to the movement of the angels between heaven and earth. Denys's account is much barer. But both Denys and Theodore are at one in their concern to interpret the *movement* of the liturgical action. There is relatively little arbitrary symbolism of the gestures and robes of the clergy and so on, that was later to form such a large part of the interpretation of the liturgy, especially in the West.

Denys sets the tone for his interpretation of the liturgical action of the Eucharist with his account of the hierarch's censing procession at the beginning of the liturgy. He proceeds out from the sanctuary, goes to the farthest point of the nave, and returns. Just so God moves outwards in procession, creating all things and drawing them into communion with himself, and does this without deserting his own unity. So too the Eucharist as a whole is a unity, and yet is 'pluralized in a sacred variegation of symbols' so as, in love, to reach out to humanity. And so, too, the bishop moves from his own contemplation of the One, out into the congregation and imparts to them what he contemplates, returning back to his contemplation without any loss.

Denys then gives a long account of the variety of ways in which the Scriptures, which are now read, communicate to us divine things and prepare us to receive them. Communication at this level is not restricted to the baptized members of the holy people. The catechumens are present and can profit from hearing the words of Scripture. But after the reading of the Scriptures they are instructed to leave, so that for the second 'more immaterial' part of the liturgy there are present only the baptized: the clergy and the laity. Then follow the Creed and the kiss of peace, a sign of the harmony amongst the members of the congregation, 'for it is not possible to be gathered together towards the One and to partake of peaceful union with the One while divided among ourselves'.

Denys summarizes the Eucharistic Prayer which, as is common in most Eastern liturgies, has a long account of man's creation and fall, and God's constant search for mankind, culminating in the coming of Christ. The reciting of the Eucharistic Prayer is, of course, the task of the bishop, and Denys concentrates the celebration of the Eucharist very much on the person of the celebrant. It is the celebrant who sings the praises of the works of God, 'those sacred works wrought gloriously by Jesus'.

> He prays that, like Christ himself, he might perform the divine things. He prays too that he might impart wisely and that all those taking part may do so without irreverence. Then he performs the most divine acts and lifts into view the things praised through the sacredly clothed symbols. (444A)

The focus on the celebrant is partly because in the central action of the Eucharist he is in some way doing what Christ did: the divine works that Christ did for us are in some way repeated by the celebrant. Another reason for the focus on the celebrant is Denys's understanding of the personal character of the passing on of sacred knowledge and communion: the hierarch himself contemplates and is united with God and the acts of his love, and it is the hierarch who extends these to the holy people.

What the celebrant effects is expressed in two ways. Firstly, he lifts up 'the things praised' so that they can be seen—something like the elevation in the Western liturgy (though there it is the host itself, unveiled, that is elevated), or rather, the showing of the holy gifts (as the Orthodox call the consecrated elements) to the people by the celebrant with the words, 'Holy things for those who are holy' (a ceremony recorded by Theodore, though not by Denys). Secondly, he distributes the consecrated bread and wine to the people in Communion. Elevation and distribution, not consecration itself: that is where Denys puts his emphasis.

> The bread which had been covered and undivided is now uncovered and divided into many parts. Similarly, he shares the one cup with all, symbolically multiplying and distributing the One in symbolic fashion. With these things he completes the most sacred act. For because of his goodness and his love for humanity the simple, hidden oneness of Jesus, the most divine Word, has taken the route of incarnation for us and, without undergoing any change, has become a reality that is composite and visible. He has beneficently accomplished for us a unifying communion with himself. (444A)

The incarnation is the revelation and movement into multiplicity of the hidden and single divinity of Jesus, out of love for men and women: and this movement is completed and made effective in the Eucharist. Denys's interest here centres on the movement of the liturgical action of taking and breaking and giving: he is much less interested in the question (which came to fascinate the West later on) of what actually happens to the sacred elements. Denys seems to take for granted that they are changed into Christ—'He offers Jesus Christ to our view'—but he says nothing about the bread and wine becoming Christ's body and blood (when he mentions the 'one body', the 'perfect, whole divine body' (444B), it is the Church that he means). The Eucharist is accomplished by being performed, and Denys keeps his attention, and ours, on the sacramental action.

THE SACRAMENT OF OIL

The ceremonies of baptism and the Eucharist that we find described in the pages of the Areopagite are much the same as those we find described by Christian Fathers in the fourth and fifth centuries. The sacrament of the oil, the sacrament that completes Denys's triad of rites or sacraments, is somewhat different. We have already observed that it is not quite a sacrament in the same way as the others: what Denys is concerned with is the consecration of the oil, not its use, whereas baptism can only take place when there are people to be baptized and the Eucharist culminates in communion; the sacrament of the oil is not confirmation, or chrismation, or anything similar. But it is puzzling in another respect: for we know nothing about it from those sources—the Mystagogical Homilies of Cyril of Jerusalem, John Chrysostom, Ambrose and Theodore of Mopsuestia—that tell us so much about the way baptism and the Eucharist were celebrated. Denys tells us about a ceremony that consists of a censing procession, followed by the singing of psalms and the reading of the Scriptures (just as in the celebration of the Eucharist: similarly, at this point the catechumens are dismissed); then the oil (*myron*: it is a mixture of oils, probably olive oil (*elaion*) and strongly fragrant oil of balsam; Denys remarks on its fragrance), in a container covered with twelve folds, is placed on the altar; the *alleluia* is sung and a prayer of consecration is offered. Nothing is known of such a ceremony, at least as early as this, in Greek or Latin sources: later on there is a solemn consecration of oils, in the West by the bishop at the morning mass on Maundy Thursday. But as has recently been shown,[13] the Syrian Orthodox Church, probably from the time of Denys himself, has known just such a 'sacrament of oil': the earliest hint of it is found in the Syrian bishop Jacob of Serugh (c. 451 – 521) and later accounts are found in Jacob of Edessa (c. 640–708) and George (c. 640–724), Bishop of the Arabians. In the Syrian Church the consecration of the oil was reserved for the patriarch, catholicos or metropolitan:[14] for Denys it is the function of the hierarch, conventionally identified with the bishop. Here, then, we have further evidence of affinity between Denys the Areopagite and the Syrian tradition.

Denys's exposition of the sacrament of the oil concentrates on two points. First, the oil symbolizes something hidden, secret, kept away from the eyes of the profane, treated with reverence and awe. The twelve folds or layers (the Greek means simply 'wings') symbolize the extreme protection of its secret hiddenness: they also symbolize the twelve wings of the seraphim, who veil the presence of God, hovering before his presence with one pair of wings, and veiling their eyes and their feet with the other two. It is then a symbol of the inner reality which the sacraments communicate to us: an inner reality only communicated to those who are ready and prepared for it. But secondly, that inner reality, the heart of the Church's sacramental life, is none other than Jesus himself. The seraphim veil the presence of God himself, and God himself, in Jesus Christ, comes to us in the incarnation. The oil is hidden, but its fragrance is perceived by all around it: the fragrance is an emanation of the hidden reality of the oil. So Denys speaks of the 'transcendent fragrance of the divine Jesus'. But in the incarnation, God becomes man. Jesus is God-made-man. Denys relates this to the fact that the sacred oil is, as we have seen, a mixture of oils (oil of balsam and olive oil in the Syrian Liturgy), and so this composite oil is a symbol of the God–man, Jesus: 'So it is that the composition of the oil is symbolic, giving a form to what is without form. It shows figuratively that Jesus is the rich source of the divine fragrances' (EH IV.iii.4: 480A).

Some have seen in this comparison between the blended oil and Jesus as God–man evidence of a Monophysite Christology[15]: we shall come back to that later. Denys's more immediate point is that it is Jesus himself who is the source of all that is derived from the sacraments: 'The divine oil is used for the consecration of any sacred thing, thereby showing clearly that, as Scripture proclaims, he who consecrates the consecrated [i.e., Jesus—cf. Heb 2:11, 13:8; Jn 17:19] remains for ever the same amid all the workings of his divine goodness' (EH IV.iii.10: 484A). Denys illustrates this by mentioning the use of oil in the service of baptism, and then adds that at the consecration of the altar oil is used: it is presumably in this way that the sacrament of oil is involved in the celebration of the Eucharist, for it is on the altar that the elements of bread and wine are consecrated and become Christ himself.[16] The sacrament of oil symbolizes the consecration that took place in the incarnation and is the source of the power of the sacraments:

> It is, so to say, the perfecting rite of God which praises in a double sense its divine work of perfection. God, first of all, having become man, was consecrated for us and, secondly, his divine act is the source of all perfection and of all consecration. (485A)

When Denys describes the anointing at the end of the ceremony of baptism, the sealing, after which the candidate is ready to take part in the Eucharist, he describes the oil as 'most theurgic'—'most deifying', perhaps (we shall discuss Denys's use of the Neoplatonic term 'theurgy' later).

THE PRIESTLY ORDERS

We have already seen how for Denys 'our hierarchy' is composed of three ranks of clergy and three ranks of laity, and that the threefold distinction of purification, illumination and perfection is shared out among the three ranks. We have also seen how very important for Denys the principle of hierarchical order is. In the chapter on the priestly hierarchy he explains how the principle of hierarchy works in the human realm: we have already dealt with that at some length (above, pp. 38–43). For the rest he gives an account of the ceremonies of ordination, which have the same basic pattern for the three ranks of the clergy with individual differences, and explains their symbolism. The elements of the ceremony are presentation at the altar, genuflexion (or maybe prostration), laying on of hands by the hierarch, sign of the cross, announcement, and kiss of peace.

We know from elsewhere[17] that it all takes place in the context of the Eucharist. There is no need here to go into the detail of Denys's symbolism. But there is one point worth making. Despite Denys's emphasis on hierarchy, it is not at all the case that such hierarchy is merely a matter of office. Though, clearly, the priestly orders derive their authority from their priestly consecration, Denys often speaks as if they derive their authority from their intrinsic, moral and intellectual qualities. He comes very close to suggesting that the efficacy of a priest's ministrations depend upon his own holiness and purity: he is very far from any Augustinian notion of the validity of orders which guarantees the efficacy of the ministry of an unworthy priest.

Part of the reason for this is historical. The Augustinian doctrine of the validity of orders was worked out in the context of the Donatist controversy in the African Church, in which the Donatist Church had broken with the Catholic Church over the issue of the value of the sacramental ministrations of a priest who had compromised with the pagan authorities during the last persecution, the so-called 'Great Persecution' under Diocletian (303–311). It was a controversy that did not have much impact in the Eastern Church where the traditional (and normal) expectation that a priest should be an example to the laity was not detached from the formal question of the source of his sacramental efficacy. The sacraments are a source of holiness: it is thus appropriate that the priest who ministers such sacraments should be holy. The Eastern Church has never worked out a formal doctrine of sacramental validity (nor involved itself in the complications it has introduced). That partly explains why Denys lays so much stress on the holiness of the priest whose ministrations are sanctifying.

But Denys's insistence seems to go further than this, and the reason is, it seems to me, that he does not see the principle of hierarchy as at all an impersonal principle. The members of the hierarchy are persons and the relationships within the hierarchy are personal relationships (like Denys's own relationship to his teacher, Hierotheus): therefore the correlation between the worth of the priest and the dignity of his office is imperative. Just as the heavenly beings are holy beings of transcendent purity who receive and pass on the rays of divine illumination, so this should be the case in the earthly hierarchy:

Therefore the founding source of all invisible and visible order quite properly arranges for the rays of divine activity to be granted first to the more godlike beings, since theirs are the more discerning minds, minds with the native ability to receive and to pass on light, and it is through their mediation that this source transmits enlightenment and reveals itself to inferior beings in proportion to their capacity. It is therefore the task of the first ranks of those beholding God to reveal fittingly and without jealousy to those of second rank the sacred sights which they behold. To initiate others into the hierarchy is the task of those who have with perfect understanding learned the divine secret of all that has to do with their hierarchy and to whom the power of sacramental initiation has been granted. It is the function of those who are full and understanding partners in clerical consecration to pass on, as appropriate, all that is sacred. (EH V.i.4: 504D–505A)

Belonging to the priestly hierarchy, like belonging at all to any rank of our hierarchy, is a response to God's call, which is itself an attraction to the divine beauty (Denys makes use of the play in Greek between *kaleō*, I call, and *kallos*, beauty). Fulfilling that call is achieved by being fashioned after the divine beauty, to be deified. The flow of divine light through the hierarchies is not a matter of impersonal power, but of a personal assimilation to God, so that the theophanous character of the created order is perfected: the more the created order is assimilated to God, the more it reflects his glory, becomes a perfect manifestation of God, a *theophany*. So the priestly order should be a group of people who share in understanding of God and his love and manifest that understanding in their lives: fundamentally their effectiveness as a priestly order is not separable from that. So Denys says of the kiss of peace in the service of ordination:

The kiss at the conclusion of the priestly consecration also has a sacred meaning. For not only do all those belonging to the priestly orders give the kiss to the initiate but so too does the consecrating hierarch. When a mind has been made sacred by the type of its priestly activity, by its call from God, by the sanctification conferred upon it, when it comes to the rite of priestly consecration, it deserves the love of its peers and of all those who belong to the most sacred orders. It has been lifted up to a beauty which brings it into full conformity with God. It has a love of like minds and enjoys their sacred love in return. So, then, this mutual priestly greeting is celebrated. It denotes the sacred communion formed by like minds and the joyous shared love which ensures for the whole hierarchy the beauty of its conformity to God. (EH V.iii.6: 513B).

THE MONK

When Denys turns to the order of the laity, his attention is mainly drawn to the highest rank of laity, the order of monks. In chapter VI he discusses the two lower orders—the order of those who need purifying, the catechumens, the penitents and the possessed, and the order of the baptized laity whom he here calls the 'contemplative order' (EH VI.iii.5: 536D 6)—but the ceremony that is described in the second part of the chapter and whose significance is drawn out in the third part is that of monastic consecration. The ceremony is relatively simple consisting of prayer, a promise on the part of the monk-to-be to be faithful and earnest in his monastic life. Then, after being marked with the sign of the cross, his hair is cut and he exchanges his clothes for others (Denys is very inexplicit about what is clearly the giving of the monastic tonsure and the clothing with the monastic habit).

By Denys's time the monastic state had achieved an important role in the life of the Church, and was to continue to exercise such a role throughout the Middle Ages and indeed, beyond, both in the East and West. But it had not always been so. In the early centuries we hear nothing about any organized Christian monasticism: it is only in the fourth century, after the Church passed from being a persecuted minority to the favoured religion of the Empire, that monasticism appears on the scene and grows rapidly.

The primary focus of this development sems to have been in Egypt. In the Egyptian Desert, the 'Desert Fathers', as they came to be called,[18] established the pattern for future monasticism. There were three types of monks: hermits, who lived a solitary life; others (semi-eremites, half-hermits) who lived what was essentially a solitary life, but lived within earshot of one another in what was known as a *lavra*; and those who lived in a community, and shared a common life of worship, eating together and working together, who were called coenobites (from *coenobium*, derived from the Greek for 'common life', *koinos bios*).[19] The life in community eventually established itself as the basic form of the monastic life: in the East the Rules of St Basil the Great provided the guidelines for this life; in the West, there were various rules, the most important being that of St Benedict (*c.* 480–*c.* 540) who must have been more or less a contemporary of our Denys.

Denys's understanding of the monastic life is concentrated on one point: the monk is a single-minded pursuer of union with unity or the One: 'Theirs is a single-minded type of life and they have the duty to

be at one only with the One, to be united with the sacred unity' (EH
VI.iii.2: 533D). We hear nothing of rules or communities or abbots
or superiors or of obedience—all an important part of monasticism
as Denys would have known it. Nor do we hear anything about
monasticism as a radical way of imitating Christ: a naked following
of the naked Christ (*nudum Christum nudus sequere*) as Jerome put
it.[20] For Denys the monastic life is characterized by unity, both as the
way and the goal. As Roques puts it, 'The monk is a solitary in
pursuit of perfect unity. While the baptized simply leads the divine
existence of the ecclesial community, the effort of the monk is
directed towards the highest perfection.'[21] Denys uses two words for
the monk, *monachos* and *therapeutēs*. 'They are called therapeutae
or monks, from the pure service and worship they offer to God, and
the single undivided lives they live as they strive for simplicity in a
sacred folding together of all division into a God-like unity and perfection of the love of God' (EH VI.i.3: 533A). The first became the
normal word for a monk in Greek (and hence in other languages),
and etymologically does suggest a solitary and thus supports Denys's
emphasis on unity. The second is an unusual word for a monk: it
only seems to occur in Denys and in the church historian Eusebius,
who uses the term because he took Philo's account of an ascetic
community in Egypt called *therapeutae* to be an account of an early
Christian community.[22] It means a servant, and Eusebius repeats
Philo's suggestion that one reason for this might be 'because of their
pure and sincere service and worship of the Divine', a hint Denys
picks up. It could be that Denys knew the passage in Eusebius, and
that the use of *therapeutēs* is part of the first-century 'colour' he
wants to give to his writings.

These two words, monk and *therapeutēs*, are not used indis-
criminately in his work. Apart from mentioning the word *therapeutēs*, Denys does not use the word at all in EH : he uses the word
'monk' and exploits its suggestions of singleness. In his letters, on
the other hand, we find that the word *therapeutēs* is used exclusively.
Five of the letters are addressed to *therapeutai*: Epp. I–IV are
addressed to one called Gaius, and Ep. VIII is addressed to Demophilus. Ep. VIII we have met several times already : not only does he
use the word *therapeutēs* to address Demophilus, it is the idea of
service, implicit in that word, that governs his presentation of the
monastic life in that epistle. Epp. I–IV are concerned to expound
particular themes discussed elsewhere in the Dionysian Corpus: Ep.
I is concerned with the 'divine darkness', Ep. II with the notion of
divine transcendence, Ep. III with the adverb 'immediately' and its

application to the incarnation, Ep. IV expounds the doctrine of the incarnation. They suggest that the monk's task is concerned with the more exalted aspects of Christian contemplation—the darkness, we have seen from MT III, is entered as we leave behind both affirmative and negative theology: they confirm what Denys says at the very beginning, that the monks are being raised 'to the most perfect perfection' (EH VI.i.3: 532D).

Clearly one reason for Denys's understanding of the monastic state as a unified state modelled on the One is because it fits very well with his Neoplatonism. All the way through the *Ecclesiastical Hierarchy* we have seen how Denys is fond of underlining how the whole orientation of the hierarchy and its ceremonies is towards unity. There is, however, another possible background for Denys's understanding of monasticism, and that lies in the Syrian tradition. There we find a tradition, older than monasticism itself, that saw the highest grade of Christian devotion in the 'single ones'. These 'single ones' (the Syriac is *ihidaya*, which can translate both *monogenēs* (only-begotten) and *monachos*) were committed to celibacy, single-mindedness, and had a special relationship to *the Ihidaya*, Christ the Only-Begotten Son. They were not organized into a monastic order, they were simply a group of deeply committed Christians and (in the fourth century) included among their numbers the two great Syriac theologians, Aphrahat and Ephrem.[23] That this is part, at least, of the background for Denys's understanding of monasticism is very attractive since, like Denys, it is an understanding of a higher stage of the Christian life revolving round the symbol of singleness or unity, and, also like Denys, it does not envisage an organized community style of life, as did later monasticism. It also ties in with the other indications of affinity between Denys and the Syrian tradition.[24]

THE RESURRECTION OF THE BODY AND THE LIFE EVERLASTING

The last chapter of the *Ecclesiastical Hierarchy* is concerned with the funeral service which gives Denys the opportunity to emphasize three things: first, the veneration of the body and the place of the body in the economy of salvation; secondly, the value of prayers for the departed; and thirdly, he defends the apparently absurd aspect of Christian liturgical ceremonies for those who do not share the

Christian faith, both in relation to Christian burial and also in relation to infant baptism.

But first let us give the form of the burial service, for this chapter like the others focuses on a ceremony in the Church's liturgy. The body of the departed is brought into the Church, a prayer of thanksgiving is said, psalms are sung and there are readings from the Scriptures (passages that relate the promise of the resurrection), the catechumens are then dismissed (but not the penitents or possessed: those who are baptized, even if they have not been faithful to their baptism, are allowed to remain), the names of the long-departed are read out and the newly-departed added to the list, and there is prayer for them all. The hierarch offers a final prayer; he then kisses the departed, and all the others present do so too. Sacred oil is poured on the body of the departed, and it is buried.

Denys lays great emphasis on the reverence that is paid to the body of the departed, for that body shared with the soul in the struggles of his earthly life and so, in the resurrection, will share in the victory (EH VII: 533A, 565B). It perhaps seems strange that, given his enormous interest in the structures of the heavenly realms and the ecclesiastical community, Denys shows little curiosity about the fate of the departed. We look forward to the resurrection; in the meantime the saints (as Denys calls all Christians, following the usage of the New Testament) 'sleep with a joyous and unshakable hope at the hour when their sacred combat ends' (EH VII.i.1: 553B). The fulfilment of the promises concerning the afterlife is beyond our understanding (560B): they speak of dwelling in 'the light in the land of the living' and being in the bosom of the patriarchs, Abraham, Isaac and Jacob. Denys sticks to such biblical language and comments that

> The bosom of the blessed patriarchs and of all the other saints signifies, I believe, this divine inheritance and this perfect beatitude where all those who have lived in conformity with God are welcomed into the ever-renewed perfection of unaging blessedness. (560 B–C)

The importance of the prayers of the saints underlines, for Denys, the fact that the Church is a community whose members all mutually support one another. Prayer for the departed is simply an extension of this mutual prayer, an extension justified by the hope of the resurrection, which manifests the Church as a community that transcends the division brought about by death. At the Eucharist, Denys tells us, the departed are regularly commemorated, 'as alive, as those who have not died but, as the Word of God teaches us, who have passed from death to a more perfectly divine life' (EH III.iii.9: 437B).

It is probably not by chance that Denys's defence of the apparent absurdity of the Christian liturgy to those who do not share the Christian faith is sparked off by his account of the Christian burial service. The pagan horror at Christian reverence for the bodies of the departed, especially the remains of the martyrs, finds eloquent expression in the account by Eunapius of Sardis of the Christianization of the pagan temples in Egypt:

> For they collected the bones and skulls of criminals who had been put to death for numerous crimes, men whom the law courts of the city had condemned to punishment, made them out to be gods, haunted their sepulchres, and thought that they became better by defiling themselves at their graves. 'Martyrs' the dead men were called, and 'ministers' of a sort, and 'ambassadors' from the gods to carry man's prayers.[25]

Eunapius (c. 345–c. 420) was a pagan Neoplatonist, and his *Lives of the Philosophers* tells us about several of the early Neoplatonists, Porphyry and Iamblichus among them. His distaste for the Christian reverence for the bodily remains of their departed would have been shared by those pagan Neoplatonists with whom Denys must be assumed to have studied. Denys defends the absurdity of Christian liturgical practices by deflecting attention from Christian burial rites to the custom of infant baptism. Here, infants who cannot understand what is going on are baptized and admitted to Communion (as still happens in the Eastern Church). Denys's defence has two prongs: first, it is not surprising the divine mysteries should be beyond our grasp; secondly, when infants are baptized, sponsors promise that they will have a godly upbringing. For Denys the supportive nature of the Christian community is so important, it is not surprising that he feels that infants born into Christian families and cared for by Christian sponsors can be, as it were, carried by the Christian community. But his point is not that the rites are unintelligible but valid, rather that understanding is a matter of degree and something that is never complete. He seems, too, to envisage a kind of dual sacramental action in which the soul is raised up to union with God by understanding the symbolism of the liturgy, and the body is prepared to be a fitting companion for the enlightened soul by the action of the material elements in the sacraments (EH

VII.iii.9: 565B): a view very similar to that found in Gregory of Nyssa's *Catechetical Oration*.[26]

THE MEANING OF THE SACRAMENTAL ACTION

Such is Denys's account of the sacramental liturgy and hierarchic structure of the Christian Church. It is a rich and fascinating account, but it leaves certain broad questions to be answered. The biggest one is perhaps this: is it not the case that this presentation of the sacraments in the context of a highly structured hierarchy, with great emphasis placed on their power of drawing Christians closer into divine union through a rich and complicated symbolism obscures, or perhaps precludes, an understanding of the sacraments as a personal encounter with Christ? What indeed is the place of Christ and the incarnation in all this? Is not the relationship between the sacraments and the incarnation obscured? Are not the sacraments being modelled so closely on Neoplatonic theurgy understood as rites and sacrifices that effect communion between the gods and men that they are being reduced to a 'sort of magical clericalism' as Jean Meyendorff has put it?[27]

It is often suggested that Denys's use of the word theurgy (*theourgia*) and its derivatives implies that he makes a distinction similar to the Neoplatonists between theology and theurgy—theology being speaking about God, theurgy being rather releasing divine power or energy—and perhaps like the later Neoplatonists, sees in theurgy a more effective way of achieving union with God (see above, p. 13). Some have suggested that his treatises can be divided into two groups that really have little in common: the *Divine Names* and *Mystical Theology* being concerned with theology, and the *Celestial Hierarchy* and *Ecclesiastical Hierarchy* being concerned with theurgy.[28]

Denys does make considerable use of *theourgia* and its derivatives, but one must not be so hasty as to suppose that he means by this word just what the Neoplatonists did. For the Neoplatonists, *theourgia* was understood as if it were the contraction of an objective genitive (work of God, *theou ergon*), that is, a work concerned with the gods: human beings accomplished a work which affected the divine realm (their understanding of this was most carefully thought-out: it did not mean that the gods were affected by what we do, rather that theurgic action made humans responsive to the divine).

73

For Denys, in contrast, *theourgia* is understood as if it were the contraction of a subjective genitive, meaning a *divine act*. Pre-eminently it means the divine acts or works that Jesus performed as incarnate. When, at the end of his account of the Scriptures that are read at the Eucharist, Denys says that 'theurgy is the consummation of theology' (EH III.iii.5: 432B), he does not mean, as we might imagine recalling some Neoplatonic utterances about theurgy, that theurgy rounds off theology, or is a more effective way of reaching God; but that the divine act in the incarnation fulfils the prophetic utterances of the Old Testament.[29]

If, with this in mind, we look at what Denys says about the various liturgical celebrations he discusses, we find that theurgy is never used to describe the liturgical action: rather, in the liturgical action, the divine work (or works) are praised or celebrated, the liturgical action itself being referred to by different words, like *hierourgia*. The liturgical actions celebrate the divine works, pre-eminently the works of Jesus the incarnate Son of God. This implies that the incarnation is much more central to the sacraments than we might have supposed. It is not at all the case that the incarnation simply effects the transition from the 'hierarchy of the Law' to 'our hierarchy', rather the incarnation and what Jesus did as incarnate is the focus of the praise and celebration in which the sacraments consist.[30] As we have seen, Jesus is the source and end of all hierarchies, hierarchy therefore is subordinated to him, insofar as he is God; though, as we have seen, as man, as Incarnate, he submits to the hierarchical arrangements he himself was responsible for. All hierarchic activity is *his* activity, as Denys makes clear especially in his exposition of the sacrament of oil. The principle of hierarchy seems at once to be a means by which all that Jesus achieved in the incarnation is made effective among men and women and available to them, but also seems to place a distance between God and mankind: there are intermediaries and their mediation is strictly observed (I nearly wrote 'jealously' but that would be wrong: as strongly as Plato, Denys emphasizes that there is no 'jealousy' in the heavenly realm; they eagerly pass on what they have received, they begrudge nothing). A final answer to this will have to await consideration of the metaphysical structure of Denys's universe.[31]

Reflection on the place of the incarnation in Denys's sacramental theology prompts one to reflect on his doctrine of the incarnation, his Christology, as such. It is obvious, when one reflects on it, that—as we would expect—Denys's ideas fit well with those current amongst those who rejected, or hesitated over, the teaching of Chalcedon out of a feeling that Cyril of Alexandria had been betrayed. In Jesus God himself is present among us: the one who is beyond being takes on human being in order to manifest himself amongst us. When he compares Jesus to the mingling of the oils to make the sacred *myron*, he uses language that would have found ready acceptance amongst Cyrillines and Monophysites. We should notice, though, that the Syriac tradition was very fond of using the imagery of 'mingling' to describe the union of the two natures of Christ.[32] Denys's most explicit Christological statement occurs in his fourth letter. Here he speaks of Jesus as God (being beyond being) out of love for humanity truly becoming man. As a result, his actions, though human actions, are also divine. He concludes by saying

> He was not a man, not as though he were not a man at all, but as one come from among men, being beyond men, he has truly become a man in a way that surpasses humanity. And for the rest, he did not do divine things divinely, or human things humanly, but as God made man, he manifested a certain new divinely-human [literally: theandric] energy, as he lived amongst us.

It was this last phrase that was quoted by Monophysites at the conference in 532—the first time we hear anything of Denys. But they misquoted it as a '*single* theandric energy': Denys is not so explicit. It is, nevertheless, difficult not to hear a rebuttal of the insistence of the *Tome of Leo*, endorsed by the Council of Chalcedon, that in the Incarnate Christ each nature 'did what was proper to it in communion with the other' (*Tome* 4), though Denys's insistence on the newness of Christ's theandric activity could be held to echo Leo's stress on the 'new order', the 'new birth', of the incarnation.[33] Denys's Christology, like that of the *Henoticon*, and that of many Eastern Christians who did not want to seem to cast doubt on the tradition of Cyril, seems ambiguous. Monophysites could appeal to it, but so too could the Orthodox: and from the time of Sophronius of Jerusalem onwards (Patriarch 634−8), Denys's idea of a 'new theandric energy' of the Incarnate One became part of the vocabulary of Orthodoxy.

Notes

1   This recalls the similar idea found in Iamblichus, *On the Mysteries of Egypt* V.18: see Rorem's note, *Works*, p. 234, n. 146.

2   Edited with Eng. trans. by A. Mingana, *Woodbrooke Studies* VI (Cambridge, 1933); and with French trans. by R. Tonneau and R. Devréesse (Studi e Testi 145; Rome, 1949).

3   *Didascalia* XIV–XVI (ed. and trans. R. H. Connolly, Oxford, 1929), pp. 130–51. And see C. H. Turner, 'Ministries of women in the primitive church . . . ' in his *Catholic and Apostolic* (ed. H. N. Bate; London and Oxford, 1931), pp. 316–51; R. Gryson, *Le Ministère des femmes dans l'Église ancienne* (Gembloux, 1972).

4   For Denys's treatment of 'our' hierarchy, see, especially, Roques, *L'Univers*, part 3, pp. 171–302.

5   Maximus the Confessor, *Mystagogia* 15 (PG 91, 693B–C).

6   EH IV.xii: 485A 15–18.

7   *Works*, p. 200, n. 17.

8   Theodore the Studite, Ep. 2.165 (PG 99, 1524B).

9   On the understanding of sacraments in Eastern Christianity, see J. Meyendorff, *Byzantine Theology* (London, 1975), pp. 191–200.

10 See Sebastian Brock, *The Luminous Eye* (Rome, 1985), p. 25.

11 For rites of initiation in the fourth/fifth century, see E. J. Yarnold, *The Awe-Inspiring Rites of Initiation* (Slough, 1971).

12 Roques, *Structures*, p. 185.

13 W. Strothmann, *Das Sakrament der Myron-Weihe in der Schrift de Ecclesiastica Hierarchia des Ps-Dionysius Areopagita* (Göttinger Orientforschungen, 1. Reihe: Syriaca 15.2; 1978), pp. xliv–xlix.

14 Ibid., p. xli.

15 Ibid., p. lx, endorsed by Rorem, *Symbols*, p. 73n.

16 As Denys says explicitly later: EH IV.i.5: 505B–C.

17 EH II.i: 425A.

18 See Benedicta Ward SLG (trans.), *The Sayings of the Desert Fathers* (London, 1975) and her introduction to *The Lives of the Desert Fathers*, trans. Norman Russell (London, 1981).

19 On this, from a vast literature, see Dom David Knowles, *Christian Monasticism* (London, 1969), and A. M. Allchin (ed.), *Solitude and Communion* (Fairacres Publications 66; Fairacres, Oxford, 1977).

20 Jerome, Ep. 125.20.

21 Roques, *Structures*, p. 224 (and see the whole of the section, 'Éléments pour une théologie de l'état monastique selon Denys l'Aréopagite', pp. 198–225).

22 See Eusebius, *Ecclesiastical History* II.17; and Philo, *On the Contemplative Life* 21–90.

23   See R. Murray, *Symbols of Church and Kingdom* (Cambridge, 1975), pp. 12–16; Sebastian Brock, *op. cit.*, pp. 107–17 (and note that, according to Brock, the Syriac translation of Eusebius's *Ecclesiastical History* brings together *ihidaya* and *therapeutēs*: p. 114).

24   To which we can add the suggestion of Sebastian Brock that Denys's interpretation of the cleansing function of the *leitourgoi* (deacons) might imply an allusion to the Syriac *mdakkyane*, though it cannot be a 'pseudo-etymology' as Denys does not use the word *diakonoi*: *op. cit.*, p. 163, n. 6.

25   Eunapius, *Lives of the Philosophers* 472 (Loeb ed., p. 425).

26   Gregory of Nyssa, *Catechetical Oration* 37 (ed. J. H. Srawley, Cambridge, 1903; p. 141, 1.1–144, 1.3).

27   J. Meyendorff, *Le Christ dans la pensée byzantine* (Paris, 1969), p. 145.

28   J. Vanneste, *Le Mystère de Dieu* (Brussels, 1959), pp. 30–5; endorsed by Meyendorff, *op. cit.*, p. 144.

29   See Rorem, *Symbols*, pp. 14f.

30   For a more detailed discussion, see my article, 'Pagan theurgy and Christian sacramentalism', *Journal of Theological Studies* 37 (1986), pp. 432–8.

31   See Roques, *L'Univers*, pp. 305–29.

32   Sebastian Brock, *op. cit.*, p. 28.

33   At the beginning of the same chapter (4) of the *Tome of Leo*.

77

5

The nameless God of
many names

The theology of Denys focuses on the liturgy. The principle of God's
movement towards men and women in transfiguring light is worked
out in his contemplation of the eternal workings of the angelic ranks
and hierarchies. How this transfiguring manifestation is realized
amongst us in the liturgical structure and liturgical activity of the
Church on earth is dwelt on at length in his discussion of 'our hierarchy'. And in all this celebration God is addressed by the praises of
men and angels. But how is God addressed? How do we use words of
him, and what do those words mean? For Denys we address God by
giving him names: or, to be more precise, not by giving him names
but by using the names that he has revealed. And to understand the
nature of God is to understand these names. But though these names
have been revealed, as names they are ways in which human meaning
is conveyed, and so they fall short of declaring the nature of God
himself. Ideas like this were commonplace in Christian theology: the
Cappadocian Fathers, especially, wrote much on the question of the
names of God, partly provoked by the claim of Eunomius, a latter-
day Arius, that the name 'unbegotten' reveals the very nature of God
(from which, therefore, the only-begotten Son is necessarily
excluded). For them God was revealed in many names, but remained
in himself beyond all names. But this theme of the 'names' of God
remained just a theme: in his *Divine Names* Denys attempted to go
further and give a systematic consideration of these names by which
we praise God. And it is made very clear that this is what we are
doing: we are purifying and perfecting our praise of God. Denys
does not speak of the names of God as merely qualities or epithets

78

that we ascribe to God: they are names with which we praise him, or celebrate or hymn him (the Greek is *hymnein*).

A SYRIAN BACKGROUND?

In composing a treatise on the names of God, Denys was not altogether original. As Sebastian Brock has pointed out, several of the hymns or songs of Ephrem the Syrian (*c.* 306–373) also take the form of a consideration of the divine names. This is especially true of the thirty-first Hymn from the cycle on the Faith, which begins:

> Let us give thanks to God who clothed himself in the names of
>   the body's various parts;
> Scripture refers to his 'ears', to teach us that he listens to us;
> It speaks of his 'eyes', to show that he sees us.
> It was just the names of such things that he put on,
> And, although in his true being there is no wrath or regret,
> Yet he put on these names, too, because of our weakness.
>
> We should realize that, had he not put on the names
> Of such things, it would not have been possible for him
> To speak with us humans. By means of what belongs to us
>   did he draw close to us:
> He clothed himself in our language, so that he might clothe us
> In his mode of life. He asked for our form and put this on,
> And then, as a father with his children, he spoke with our
>   childish state.[1]

Ephrem mentions some of the names God put on—Old Man, Ancient of Days, Valiant Warrior—and goes on to compare God's revealing himself to man, with a man teaching a parrot to talk:

> A person who is teaching a parrot to speak
> Hides behind a mirror and teaches it in this way:
> When the bird turns in the direction of the voice which is
>   speaking,
> It finds in front of its eyes its own resemblance reflected;
> It imagines that it is another parrot conversing with itself.
> The man puts the bird's image in front of it, so that thereby it
>   might learn how to speak.
>
> This bird is a fellow creature with the man,
> But although this relationship exists, the man beguiles and
>   teaches

> The parrot something alien to itself by means of itself; in this
>   way he speaks with it.
> The divine Being that in all things is exalted above all things
> In his love bent down from on high and acquired from us our
>   own habits:
> He laboured by every means so as to turn us all to himself.[2]

Ephrem's humorous analogy conveys well the vast disparity between God and man which is bridged by God's revealing himself. There are, according to Ephrem, two kinds of names that God puts on: 'perfect and exact names' and 'borrowed names'. 'Perfect and exact names' indicate something of his true nature; 'borrowed' names are metaphors drawn from human experience. Examples of perfect names are 'Being', 'Creator', 'Father', 'Son', and 'Holy Spirit': without these there can be no conception at all of the divine nature.

> Take care of God's perfect and holy names,
> For if you deny one of them, then they all fly away off:
> Each one is bound up with the other,
> They support everything, like the pillars of the world.[3]

Even when these 'perfect' names are names that are also used of humans, their primary meaning is divine, it is their human use that is 'borrowed'. So Ephrem explains that people

> . . . have been called 'gods', but he is God of all;
> They are called 'fathers', but he is the True Father;
> They are named 'spirits', but that is the Living Spirit.
> The terms 'father' and 'son' by which they have been called
> Are borrowed names that through grace have taught us
> That there is a Single True Father
> And that he has a single True Son.[4]

In the 'perfect names' there takes place the most exalted encounter between human beings and God: by pondering them we are drawn close to God himself. The 'borrowed' names God has put on in his love of mankind, in order to draw men and women up to him.

There are parallels to all this in Denys's *Divine Names*. Especially in the first chapter he speaks of the innumerable names by which God is praised in the Scriptures. And the purpose of these names, as with Ephrem, is not just to reveal something *about* God, but to draw men and women into union with God: to deify them. 'When, for instance, we give the name of "God" to that transcendent hiddenness, when we call it "life" or "being" or "light" or "Word", what our minds lay hold of is in fact nothing other than certain activities apparent to us, activities which deify, cause being, bear life, and give wisdom' (DN II.7).

But there is much in Denys's treatment of the divine names that seems very different from Ephrem. He has, for instance, no real parallel to Ephrem's distinction between 'perfect' and 'borrowed' names: his classification of the divine names proceeds on quite other lines. He distinguishes between names expressive of concepts and names drawn from the realm of the senses: these latter names belong to 'symbolic theology', the former are the concern of the treatise, the *Divine Names* (DN I.8). He maintains, like Ephrem, that names like 'father' and 'son' apply properly to God and to human beings only in a secondary sense (DN II.8): but this had been a commonplace of Christian theology from the time of the Arian controversy.[5] We have already seen that there is a good deal of evidence that Denys's background is partly that of Syrian Christianity, and it is tempting to see further evidence here. It may well be that Ephrem's outlines of a treatment of the names of God inspired him: but there are other influences on Denys's treatment of the divine names that seem more important.

NEOPLATONIC TEACHING ON THE DIVINE NAMES

It is to Neoplatonic influences that we must turn for a more immediate background to the *Divine Names*. The Neoplatonists were also interested in working out a doctrine of the divine by considering divine names. Though what Denys *says* he is doing (namely, investigating the names given to God in the Scriptures) draws him very close to Ephrem, what he actually does betrays his deep affinity with Neoplatonism. After three introductory chapters, Denys settles down to a systematic discussion of divine names, beginning with the 'Good' and ending with the 'One'. After the chapter on the Good, there follow three chapters on 'Being', 'Life' and 'Wisdom', which echo Proclus's triad, Being–Life–Intelligence. All that suggests a strongly Neoplatonic ambiance. In the rest of the treatise, some names treated are clearly scriptural (e.g., 'Almighty', 'Ancient of Days' in DN X; 'Holy of Holies', 'King of Kings' etc. in DN XII), others have both biblical and Neoplatonic echoes ('Power' in DN VIII; 'Peace' in DN XI) and still others seem only explicable against a Neoplatonic background. The instances in this latter category are instructive. DN IX is concerned with 'greatness and smallness, sameness and difference, likeness and unlikeness, rest, motion, and equality', and although Denys produces biblical references, it all seems puzzling unless one realizes that these qualities are precisely the qualities discussed as attributes of the One in the Neoplatonic interpretation of the series of hypotheses found in the second part of Plato's dialogue, *Parmenides* (137C–166C). Two other divine names (discussed in DN X) are 'eternity' (*aiōn*) and 'time' (*chronos*). Plotinus himself had not regarded these as substantive principles, but Proclus did; and E. R. Dodds remarked in his commentary on Proclus's *Elements of Theology*, 'I suspect that Proclus had a special reason for hypostatizing *aiōn* and *chronos*, namely their importance in late Hellenistic cultus and contemporary magic'.[6]

It is necessary here to say a word about the treatment of the divine names in Neoplatonism: it will both help us to understand Denys and to appreciate his originality in relation to Neoplatonism. For the Neoplatonists, the divine names are the names of the *gods*: so, for instance, as Dodds's quotation above implies, *Aiōn* and *Chronos* refer to gods. For Plato himself there had been an almost complete divorce between philosophy and religious mythology, the latter containing absurd and scandalous stories of supposedly divine beings, while philosophy concerned itself with truth of an entirely different order. Part of the inspiration of Neoplatonism, however, was a conviction that the ancient religious traditions of the Greeks were genuine (if veiled) revelations of the divine, and a succession of Neoplatonic philosophers endeavoured to reconcile Greek mythology with the more austere understanding of the divine found in the Platonic dialogues. This was achieved by a combination of allegory (applied to the myths) and commentary (applied to the Platonic dialogues). One dialogue that proved to be particularly fruitful was Plato's *Parmenides*. In this dialogue the aged Eleatic philosopher, Parmenides, encounters the youthful Socrates. In the first part of the dialogue, Parmenides subjects the theory of the Forms to searching criticisms; in the second part he engages in deductive arguments based on various hypotheses concerning the one (or the One, or 'one thing'). Many Platonists had regarded this section as a logical exercise in deductive argument (for example, Albinus in the second century AD[7]), and it was (or had been) a sufficiently influential position for Proclus to go to the trouble of refuting it in his *Platonic Theology*.[8] The Neoplatonists, however, thought it incredible that so much time should be spent on a mere logical exercise, and regarded it as a treatise on theology: the first hypothesis was understood to refer to the One, which is absolutely one and utterly simple, and the argument shows that it follows from this that nothing at all can be said about the One; the second argument varies the hypothesis to 'if the One is', that is, if it participates in being and so is not absolutely one, and on this basis various attributes are ascribed to the One, and so on. These attributes are regarded as *divine* attributes: attributes ascribed to the One as it manifests itself at the various levels of reality. The gods to whom these divine names refer are identified with the gods of Greek mythology by means of allegory (for example, Mount Ida refers to the lofty realm of the ideas; difference, unlikeness and so on are manifest in the stories of the battles of the gods).

In fact, in the fully developed form we find in Proclus (especially in his *Platonic Theology*) it is even more complicated than this. We have already seen that Plotinus had distinguished between three hypostases—the One, Intelligence, and Soul—and saw them related by a downward movement of procession and an answering movement of return. Since the levels of Intelligence and Soul admit of multiplicity, it was possible to distinguish between Intelligence and intelligences (or minds) and Soul and souls: individual souls participate in the hypostasis Soul and individual minds in the hypostasis Intelligence. They realize the original reality in particular forms. The realm of minds possesses a unity which is realized in Mind or Intelligence; the realm of soul possesses a unity which is realized in Soul. As the individual soul withdraws into itself, it realizes a kinship with all other souls, and as it 'returns' to the intuitive state of intelligence, it becomes intelligence itself ('we are each of us the intelligible world', as Plotinus had put it).[9] But how does the One relate to what comes after it? How does mind emanate from the One? It is the hardest problem of Plotinus's philosophy: any link between the absolutely transcendent One and the many seems to compromise the very nature of the One. One begins to see how the *Parmenides* could be so fascinating to Neoplatonists: by considering different ways in which the One could be, it seems to suggest some kind of path from absolute One to a unity composed of multiplicity.

In Proclus's system (the idea seems to go back to his master, Syrianus) these ideas are incorporated by postulating unities (Greek: *henades*, anglicized as 'henads') alongside the One, just as there are intelligences alongside Intelligence and souls alongside Soul. The henads exist alongside the One and replicate unity without destroying it.[10] The One itself remains utterly transcendent: nothing can be said of it save that it is One (which means that it is the sole source of all that is) and that it is Good (meaning the ultimate goal of all that is). The henads are (ultimately) the recipients of the divine attributes or names yielded by the later hypotheses of the *Parmenides*, and by the other Platonic dialogues. For it is not the *Parmenides* alone that yields a doctrine of divine attributes: Proclus finds them discussed in many other dialogues. A notable example is the famous analogy of the sun in the *Republic*. The sun, which is transcendent over the visible world and by its light makes both knowledge and life possible, is presented by Socrates as an analogy of the Good (or form of the Good) which is transcendent over the world of understanding (indeed 'beyond being and knowledge') and by its influence (its 'light') gives being and knowledge to that world. In the *Platonic Theology*, Proclus supports his exposition of the *Parmenides* by referring to the analogy of the sun and regards the two sequences—One–divinity–henads–intelligibles (derived from the *Parmenides*) and Good–light–gods–intelligibles (derived from the *Republic*)—as identical.[11]

What this means is that the process of emanation from the One, which is the source of all reality, through Intelligence and Soul, is to be seen in a more complex way, whereby the multiplicity that is the result of emanation can be traced back to the level of the One in the henads: so one can think equally of emanation from the One or emanation from the henads. The advantages of the second way of thinking are (philosophically) that the manifold, belonging to (or manifested in) the henads, is not illusory, and (religiously) that all that is, and the governance of all that is (providence), can be ascribed to the gods. The first way of thinking (of emanation from the One itself) is more ultimately true: to think like that is to pass beyond the knowable into the realm of the unknowable.

DENYS'S CORRECTIVE TO NEOPLATONISM

The danger of Neoplatonism for Denys and Christianity is, then, very great. It is not just that a doctrine of emanation may tend to obscure the fundamental difference between the Being of God and the being of creatures, it is rather that the whole analysis of reality that Proclus offers subserves a polytheistic religious system. Denys, attracted by the subtlety of the Neoplatonic analysis of reality, must strive as a Christian to block off those aspects of the system that open the door to a doctrine of many gods.

Denys does this in two ways, which are, I think, ultimately equivalent: first, he qualifies the notion of emanation by insisting that being is derived from God alone; and secondly, he turns the doctrine of divine names into a doctrine of divine attributes (that is, attributes of God, the one God). Emanation, in a Neoplatonic sense, is a doctrine about the derivation of *being*: being derives from the One, but in the stream of emanated beings, each being receives from the one above it (actually for Proclus, beings that are capable of self-presence, that is, self-conscious beings, are identical with that from which they proceed, and so are in a way self-created)—creation is not restricted to the One, the whole realm of being that flows from the One is creative. Denys takes over the Neoplatonic idea of a scale of being, and also the idea that lower beings are dependent on higher beings, but he rejects any idea that being is (as it were) passed down this scale of being: all beings are created immediately by God.[12] The scale of being and the sense of dependence only has significance in the matter of *illumination*: light and knowledge flow from God down through the scale of being—each being becomes radiant with light and thus passes on light to beings lower down.

It is perhaps this understanding of emanation simply in terms of illumination and not communication of being, that explains Denys's fondness for the analogy of the sun (referred to: DN IV.1, IV.5, V.8), though for Plato, as we have seen, the sun (and therefore the Good) is regarded as the source not just of knowledge, but of life (and being). Strikingly, though, Denys does not speak much of creation; he is more interested in the interrelationships of the created order, and never speaks of creation *ex nihilo*, even though by this time the idea of creation out of nothing had become the normal and accepted way in which Christians expressed their belief in creation: he prefers to say that we come from (*ek*) God, than from nothing.[13] The reason for this is that creation is not central to his understanding of the relationship of the universe to God (though it is true). But neither is emanation central. We have to find another word for what it is that is central to Denys's understanding of God's relationship to the world: and a good candidate for that word would be *theophany*. The world is a theophany, a manifestation of God, in which beings closer to God manifest God to those further away. The world is God's glory made manifest: it exists to display his glory and draw everything into contemplation of his beauty. The doctrine of creation is necessary to such an understanding of the world as theophany: God is immediately present to his whole creation as its creator; created reality is not, as created, an obstacle to his glory, neither because it owes its being to something other than (or even alien to) God, nor because it is an increasingly remote echo of God's original creative urge. But if God is to manifest himself outside himself, that implies multiplicity, which in turn implies difference, which must be either ordered or disordered: and for Denys, only an ordered, hierarchical creation could manifest the glory of the One.[14]

Denys's other modification of the Neoplatonic doctrine of divine names is to insist that they are simply divine attributes, that is, attributes of the one God. This is another way of saying that being only proceeds from God or the One, the modification of the doctrine of emanation that we have just discussed. The divine attributes display the manifold splendour of God's self-manifestation, but they do not have their proper signification in applying to exalted beings who have emanated from God. The divine attributes do not ultimately refer to the henads. In part this is implicit: Denys simply assumes as a Christian that there is only one God. But it is occasionally made quite explicit. In DN XI Denys discusses a query from Timothy about the use of expressions like 'life itself' (that is, the essence of life, or, in Platonic terms, the form or Idea of life). Sometimes they are applied to God, sometimes they are said to be caused by God. In his reply Denys explicitly counters the Neoplatonic understanding of this:

> The absolute being underlying individual manifestations of being as their cause is not a divine or angelic being, for only transcendent being itself can be the source, the being, and the cause of the being of beings. Nor have we to do with some other life-producing divinity distinct from that supra-divine life which is the originating cause of all living beings and of life itself. Nor, in summary, is God to be thought of as identical with those originating and creative beings and substances which men stupidly describe as certain gods or creators of the world. Such men, and their fathers before them, had no genuine or proper knowledge of beings of this kind. Indeed, there are no such beings. What I am trying to express is something quite different. 'Being itself', 'life itself', 'divinity itself' are names dignifying source, divinity, and cause, and these are applied to the one transcendent cause and source beyond the source of all things. But we use the same terms in a derivative fashion and we apply them to the provident acts of power which come forth from that God in whom nothing at all participates . . . [15]

Instead of a distinction between the One and the gods, Denys has a somewhat different distinction in that 'being itself', etc., are applied to God, but in two ways: either to God himself, or to his activity in the world. Denys's distinction recalls (or rather foreshadows) the distinction between the essence and energies of God, found in St Gregory Palamas (c. 1296–1359) and other late Byzantine (and indeed modern Orthodox) theologians.

But this example reveals an untidiness (or, perhaps, a paradox) in Dionysian theology, in contrast to Neoplatonism. Denys is here trying to explain how God can be regarded *both* as 'being itself' *and* as the source of 'being itself'. This contradiction was reconciled in Procline Neoplatonism by applying these different terms to different entities. The source of all, beyond any attribute, is the One; the attributes are then applied to different beings who proceed from the One, the henads. In place of such logical simplicity (although complicated in other ways), Denys wants to speak of the attributes of One who is beyond all attribution.

APOPHATIC AND CATAPHATIC THEOLOGY

This can be put in another way. We have seen the importance for late Neoplatonism of the interpretation of the successive hypotheses of the second part of the *Parmenides*: the first hypothesis yields the One of whom nothing at all can be said, the succeeding hypotheses yield manifestations of the divine of whom something can be said. There is a neat distinction between apophatic theology (that is, theology of denial) and cataphatic theology (that is, theology of affirmation): apophatic theology applies to the One, cataphatic theology to the henads and other divine manifestations of the One. The terms 'apophatic' and 'cataphatic' theology become familiar terms in Byzantine theology, from the time of Maximus the Confessor and John Damascene (c. 650–c. 750). Their first Christian use seems to be in Denys: but they are also used freely in a theological context by Proclus. For Denys, however, the reference of both apophatic and cataphatic theology is the One God: they are apparently contradictory or paradoxical. It is of the same God that we are to make both affirmations and denials. Denys has, as it were, identified the hypotheses of the *Parmenides* (or rather the first two hypotheses). What Procline Neoplatonism kept, logically and ontologically, apart, Denys brings together in stark paradox. God reveals something of himself. We can affirm that: this is cataphatic theology. But what God reveals of himself is not himself; as we seek to understand God as he is in himself, we must go behind the affirmations we make, and deny them of God, and thus engage in apophatic theology. It is apophatic theology that is the more ultimate: our denials are truer than our affirmations in relation to God. So, for instance, Denys can say,

> Therefore God is known in all things and apart from all things; and God is known by knowledge and by unknowing. Of him there is understanding, reason, knowledge, touch, perception, opinion, imagination, name and many other things, but he is not understood, nothing can be said of him, he cannot be named. He is not one of the things that are, nor is he known in any of the things that are; he is all things in everything and nothing in anything; he is known to all from all things and to no-one from anything. For we rightly say these things of God, and he is celebrated by all beings according to the analogy that all things bear to him as their Cause. But the most divine knowledge of God, that in which he is known through unknowing, according to the union that transcends the mind, happens when the mind, turning away from all things, including itself, is united with the dazzling rays, and there and then illuminated in the unsearchable depth of wisdom. (DN VII.3: 872A–B)

Apophatic and cataphatic theology apply to the One God and represent the movement by which the intellect grasps God's revelation of himself by affirming it, and then penetrates beyond knowledge about God to God himself, by denying and transcending what he has revealed of himself. The successive chapters of the *Divine Names* explore this movement by which the soul is divinized, in relation to the various attributes of God.

THE DOCTRINE OF THE TRINITY

The first three chapters of the *Divine Names* provide a preface to the treatment of the divine names. As we have already mentioned, they seem to contain a summary of the contents of the *Theological Outlines*, namely the doctrines of the Trinity and the incarnation.[16] Before discussing the names through which God has revealed his being, Denys expounds the names through which God has revealed something of his inner life. What Denys has to say about the Trinity (and even more briefly, the incarnation) belongs to the tradition of Greek Patristic theology, especially as we find it in the Cappadocian Fathers, but he expresses it in language that draws heavily on the vocabulary of Neoplatonism (though it might be doubted whether this use of philosophical terminology makes for much clarity).

Denys introduces a distinction between union (*henōsis*) and differentiation (*diakrisis*): some names of God have to do with union (or 'are unified'), others have to do with differentiation ('are differentiated'). The 'unified names' apply to the whole Godhead (he occasionally calls them 'common' names, using the expression the Cappadocian Fathers used): such names are being, unity, goodness, etc. They apply equally to each of the Persons of the Trinity (DN II.3). The 'differentiated names'—such as Father, Son and Holy Spirit—do not apply to the whole Godhead, but to the individual Persons of the Trinity, and cannot be interchanged (DN II.5). Thus far we have nothing more than the concepts of the Cappadocian Fathers couched in unfamiliar language. Denys, however, has a little more to say (not nearly enough, alas: for more detail he refers to the lost *Theological Outlines*). The unions, we are told, are 'the hidden and inseparable supreme foundations of a permanence which is beyond ineffability and unknowing'; the differentiations are 'the benign processions and manifestations of the Thearchy' (DN II.4: 640D). 'Unions', then, refer to the One, either by referring to the utterly ineffable source of all, that the One is (the word translated 'permanence', *monimotēs*, may be intended to convey an allusion to *monē*, rest, the first term of the triad, rest–procession–return), or by referring to the movement of return, which is unifying or simplifying. Either way, we are immersed in Neoplatonism (in Proclus, the latter use is perhaps more common, while, for Denys, the former seems more central). Similarly, differentiation means emanation or procession (which is Proclus's definition of *diakrisis*[17]). However, Denys wants something more complex than Neoplatonism, where differentiation is simply the consequence (or meaning) of procession, and union the goal and method of return. He goes on to say that there are some names that are proper to union, and also some unions and differentiations that are proper to differentiation. What is proper to union are the common names—being, divinity, goodness, etc.—which are united and common to the 'indivisible Trinity', and also the 'rest and establishment in one another of the indivisible Persons'. He compares these unified qualities to the light in a single room where there are several lamps. The light that shines from the room is one and undivided: here there are 'things united in differentiation and things differentiated in union' (641A–B). All this seems to suggest that the indivisibility of the Trinity is both expressed in the fact that the divine attributes (or divine activities) cannot be distributed amongst the Persons of the Trinity, and also is to be found in the mutual indwelling of the Persons of the Trinity (what was later to be called *perichōrēsis*, or coinherence: St John Damascene, whose *Exposition of the Faith* first popularized the language of *perichōrēsis* in Byzantine theology, does so in language which is deeply indebted to the Areopagite[18]). Denys then says that differentiation in speaking of God who is beyond being is applied in two ways: either to the names we give to the Persons that distinguish them ('Father' and 'Son', for instance) or to the way in which God manifests himself in creation as being, life, wisdom, etc., so as to share these properties (and ultimately divinity itself) with the whole created order (DN II.50). So union and differentiation can be conceived of in two different ways. There are 'unified names' which refer to the whole indivisible Godhead: as a result of differentiation ('the generous procession of divine unity overflowing with goodness in a way that transcendently preserves unity and making itself manifold') these manifestations of God flow into the world, manifesting the divine and stirring up beings to return to the One. There are 'differentiated names' which refer to the Persons of the Trinity: these differentiations are contained within the unity of the Godhead. Another example of differentiation is the incarnation, for this refers to the Person of the Word (or the Son) and not to the Father or the Spirit (644C): Denys refers to this a little later on, to profess its utter ineffability (DN II.9: 648A). It is, however, clearly something quite different from God's manifestation of himself through the divine names.

If we try and put all this together, we seem to have the idea that God manifests his whole being in attributes (or names) which we grasp as they are differentiated from God in their procession or radiation from him. There is also the idea that within the Godhead there is some kind of primordial procession in which 'the Father is the originating Source of the Godhead, and the Son and the Spirit are divine shoots, and, as it were, flowers and transcendent lights of the divinely fruitful divinity' (DN II.7). (The Father as 'originating source of Godhead' is not far from the Cappadocian idea of the Father as 'source of divinity'; the rest of the language is reminiscent of the Chaldaean Oracles, doubtless transmitted through Proclus.) In the incarnation, it seems, this primordial procession is manifest in the world of creation. The use of the language of procession (if it is not just fashionable late fifth-century language, and confusing as fashions often are) raises problems that Denys does not answer. Procession is logically inferior to the unity from which it proceeds: Denys himself says that 'in divine matters unions are more important than differentiations' (DN II.11: 652A). Does this mean that the Unity within the Godhead is in some sense prior to, more ultimate than, the Trinity of Persons? Sometimes Denys seems to indicate that this is far from what he means, and it would certainly be far from the trinitarian theology of the Cappadocian Fathers. For instance, he says

> For the Unity that is celebrated, and the Trinity which is beyond all divinity, is not unity or trinity in any of our senses of the words, but in order to praise truly the transcendent unity and divine fruitfulness, we call the One beyond all names, whose being transcends all beings, with the divine names of Trinity and Unity. (DN XIII.3: 980D–981A)

God is not Unity beyond Trinity, but beyond both Unity and Trinity in any way that we can understand these terms: Unity and Trinity, it would seem, are equally ultimate, and equally transcended. But the idea of a Godhead beyond the Trinity is at least suggested by Denys's language, even though it is a suggestion he seems not to take up himself: the suggestion was certainly taken up by others, for instance, in the late Middle Ages by Meister Eckhart, with his notion of 'God beyond God'.[19]

PRAYER

Denys's exposition of the doctrine of the Trinity is presented only in summary form and as a preface to the main body of the work, a systematic treatment of the divine names. Before he embarks on this, however, he turns in prayer to the Holy Trinity and reflects on the nature of prayer itself. In prayer we are drawn into the divine presence, not as if the divine became present when before he was not, but in our turning to him we realize his presence within us. He gives two vivid analogies of what he means:

> It is as if there were a great chain of light let down from the summit of the heavens and reaching down to the earth, and as we grasp it first with one hand, then another, we seem to be

drawing it down, but really it remains there and it is we who are being raised up to the most exalted splendours of its shining rays. Or it is as if we were on a boat pulling on ropes thrown across from a rock to help us: we do not draw the rock towards us, but ourselves and the boat to the rock . . . (DN III.1: 680C)

Such an understanding of prayer had been commonplace in the Christian tradition,[20] but it was commonplace, too, among Neoplatonists: prayer, as it were, makes conscious the reality of our relationship to what is higher, what is ultimate. As such it has been called 'ontological prayer', prayer which expresses the nature of our ontological condition.[21]

THE STRUCTURE OF THE *DIVINE NAMES*

Denys now embarks on his systematic treatment of the divine names. These names, we have seen, begin with the Good and end with the One. A good deal of ingenuity has been expended on the question of the structure of the *Divine Names*. As we have it now, it begins with some intelligible order, with the Procline triad, being–life–intelligence, providing the basis for the next three chapters after the chapter on the Good (DN IV): Being (DN V), Life (DN VI), Wisdom (DN VII). After that any order seems less clear. A rearrangement of the chapters (first suggested by Endre von Ivánka[22]) finds in the *Divine Names* a reference to the names of the churches built in Constantine's new capital, Constantinople: the churches of the Holy Wisdom (*Haghia Sophia*), of Holy Power (*Haghia Dynamis*), and of Holy Peace (*Haghia Eirēnē*). If chapter XI is transposed to follow chapter VIII, then the chapters following chapter IV (on the Good) treat successively two triads: the Procline triad, being–life–wisdom, and the 'Constantinopolitan' triad, wisdom–peace–power (the two triads overlapping in DN VII). Then would follow the chapter on the 'Parmenidean' attributes (the present chapter IX: Ivánka regards the present chapter X as a biblical appendix to that) and then the final chapter on the One (the present chapter XII Ivánka regards as having been introduced as a transition between the chapters on Peace and the One, when DN XI was transferred to its present position). Ivánka's ideas are quite hypothetical, and there are reasons for being sceptical about them;[23] nonetheless, he has found favour with some scholars, for instance I. P. Sheldon-Williams, who would summarize the doctrine of the

Divine Names as the Divine Goodness, itself ineffable, making itself known at the level of intelligence as Being, Life, and Intelligence; in the soul as Wisdom, Power, and Peace; and in the physical world as Holy of Holies, Lord of Lords, King of Kings, and God of Gods.[24]

Whatever the structure of the treatise, the treatment of the divine names provides, on the one hand, a series of illustrations of the inter-relationship between cataphatic and apophatic theology—each chapter expounds what is revealed and then beckons the mind to ascend still further by denial of what is revealed—and, on the other, the opportunity for a rather piecemeal exposition of various meta-physical themes fundamental to Denys's understanding of the universe. We have already dwelt on the former; it remains to treat some of the latter themes. The longest chapter by far is chapter IV on the Good: this contains a long discussion of the problem of evil (which is closely dependent on a treatise by Proclus, and solves the problem of evil by identifying evil with non-being), but also introduces a number of important ideas, notably providence and love, which will provide the starting-point for the rest of this chapter.

PROVIDENCE

The notion of providence (*pronoia*) casts a long shadow over Denys's thought: he rarely talks about it explicitly,[25] but he very frequently speaks of the divine influence (in its many forms) as being 'providential' (*pronoētikos*). Such an emphasis on providence is yet another sign of his affinity with Neoplatonism. For Plato, to deny that the gods exercise providence was a blasphemy drawing upon itself the gravest punishment;[26] later Platonists defended the notion of providence against the idea of fate with which the Stoics and others identified it. In Neoplatonism, providence is a dimension of the notion of procession: lower beings do not simply proceed from the One and the henads, but are the object of the providence of the henads. Proclus derives the term *pronoia* from 'before mind' (*pro nou*) and sees in it the transcendent form of intelligence found amongst the gods.[27] It is, as it were, the original of which thought and reasoning in minds and souls are a copy or an echo: providence contains within itself the meaning that is discerned at lower levels by thought and reasoning.[28] Providence, or *pronoia*, characterizes very generally the relation of the henads to lower levels of reality.

All this deeply colours Denys's thought and language: the 'providential rays' that shine forth from God communicate his manifestation within the world. God manifests himself through his attributes, his names, and these unfold his providential care for the world. Denys speaks, too, of 'paradigms' (DN V.8–10) which seem to be the divine attributes perceived in their relation to creation: as the attributes reveal aspects of the unknowable Godhead, so, as paradigms, they are archetypes for creaturely reality.[29] What philosophy calls paradigms, theology calls predeterminations (*proorismoi*), or 'divine and good wills': they are the forms that God's pre-intelligence (*pronoia*) determines. 'Starting from being, from the procession of goodness that is productive of being, moving through all things and filling all things with a gift of itself, and rejoicing in all that is, it anticipates all things in itself . . . ' (DN V.9: 825A). And the point of these paradigms, or predeterminations, or divine and holy wills, is to reveal God in such a way that we may be raised up to union with him: 'so that through the knowledge we have of the source of all through the analogy of these things, we are to be raised up as far as possible'. We are deified, so to speak, by being identified with the paradigm or predetermination God has determined for us: one with God's will for us, we express perfectly God's intention, and radiate limpidly the divine light that we have received. E. R. Dodds remarked that 'the topic of *pronoia* bulks almost as large in Neoplatonism as does that of predestination and grace in the Christian theology of the period'.[30] It was, however, only in Christian theology in the West that predestination and grace loomed large; in the East categories similar to those of Neoplatonism (Origenist, Evagrian, and later Dionysian) were prominent: we can see from this brief outline something of the difference of emphasis it entailed. Providence makes room for the response of human freewill more easily than does the Augustinian doctrine of grace and predestination.

LOVE

A particularly striking way in which Denys speaks of providence is when he considers the divine name, Good, under the aspect of love (*erōs* or *agapē*, which he argues, following patristic precedent, to be equivalent). God creates the world out of his goodness, or out of his love. And love is defined as essentially 'ecstatic', that is: the one who loves is drawn out of himself and centres his being on the object of his love. Love is ecstatic, because it is unitive: the lover is united to the beloved, who is, for him, a manifestation of beauty. For love is 'a power that unites and binds together and effects an indissoluble fusion in the beautiful and the good' (DN IV.12: 709C). But love is not for Denys mainly a matter of our striving for God: it is essentially something divine, and when we love God, we love him with his love. But since it is essentially divine, we can speak of God's love, and indeed of God's ecstatic love:

> We must dare add this as being no less true: that the Source of all things himself, in his wonderful and good love for all things, through the excess of his loving goodness, is carried outside himself, in his providential care for all that is, so enchanted is he in goodness and love and longing. Removed from his position above all and beyond all he descends to be in all according to an ecstatic and transcendent power which is yet inseparable from himself. (DN IV.13: 712A–B)

The idea of a divine 'providential love' (*erōs pronoētikos*) is found in Proclus, but not the idea of God's 'ecstatic' love. Nor is Proclus's divine 'providential love' quite the same as Denys's notion of God's 'providential love', for *Erōs* is *one* of the gods for Proclus, and not indeed one of the highest of them.[31] John Rist's comment is to the point:

> The first person to combine the Neoplatonic idea about God as Eros with the notion of God's 'ecstasy' is Pseudo-Dionysius, and it would seem merely perverse to deny that Dionysius' Christianity is the direct cause of this adaptation. Dionysius has in fact adapted Eros to the Christian demand that God love all things, and he is the first person to do so.[32]

What we have in Denys is really a transformation of the Greek notion of *erōs*: for Plato *erōs* primarily (though not exclusively) met a need, and the neediness of love remains in the pagan Greek tradition; for Denys *erōs*, yearning love, is an overflow of divine goodness—it needs nothing, it is the source of everything.

The way in which love, though mentioned only briefly in DN IV, has deeply coloured Denys's understanding of reality can be seen in his treatment of the twin names, Power and Peace, for love is a force as powerful as anything we know and its goal is unity. So Denys waxes his most eloquent as he hymns the name, Power:

> It preserves the immortal lives of the angelic henads unharmed and the heavens and the luminous starry beings and their orders unchangeable . . . it makes the power of fire unquenchable and the flow of water unfailing . . . it protects the

indissoluble abiding of the universe; to those made godlike it grants the power of deification itself. (DN VIII.5: 829D–893A)

But the power of deification is the power of union and harmony: the power of peace. For peace is the longing of all things: Denys affirms this as strongly as Augustine.[33] And the perfection of peace is a harmony that preserves the distinctiveness and individuality of all:

> And perfect peace guards the unmingled individuality of each, with its peaceful providence ensuring that all things are free from disturbance and confusion both within themselves and amongst themselves, holding all things in peace and rest by a stable and unshakeable power. (DN XI.3: 952C)

THE ONE

The last chapter of the *Divine Names* leads us back to the name, the One, which is not only the source and goal of all things, but, as we have seen, one of Denys's favourite terms for God. It provides an opportunity for summing up much that he has said about the essential role of unity in the nature of reality. But the absolute nature of the One implies that it is beyond any kind of attribution, and so the *Divine Names* ends by reminding us of the greater ultimacy of apophatic over cataphatic theology:

> But they [sc. the theologians, the Scriptural writers] prefer the ascent through negations. This way draws the soul out of what is connatural to it, and leads it through all divine conceptions which are transcended by the One that is beyond every name and all reason and knowledge, and brings it into contact with Him beyond the uttermost boundaries of the universe, insofar as such contact is possible to us. (DN XIII.3: 981B)

Notes

1 Ephrem, *Hymn 31 on the Faith*, 1f. (ed. E. Beck, *Corpus Scriptorum Christianorum Orientalium* 154 (Scriptores Syri 73; Louvain, 1955), pp. 105ff.): trans. in Sebastian Brock, *The Luminous Eye* (Rome, 1985), pp. 43f.: see the whole section ('The garment of names'), pp. 43–8.

2 *Hymn 31*, 6f. (ed. Beck, pp. 106f.): trans. pp. 44f.

3   *Hymn 44 on the Faith*, 3 (ed. Beck, p. 141): trans., p. 46.

4   *Hymn 46 on the Faith*, 12 (ed. Beck, pp. 148f.): trans., pp. 46f.

5   See, e.g., Athanasius, *Against the Arians* I.21.

6   E. R. Dodds (ed.), *Proclus: The Elements of Theology* (2nd ed., Oxford, 1963), p. 228: Dodds goes on to give examples of their importance in such circles.

7   Or Alcinous, the author of the *Didaskalikos*, an introduction to Platonic philosophy.

8   Proclus, *Platonic Theology* I.9 (ed. H. D. Saffrey and L. G. Westerink, Paris, 1968, pp. 34–40).

9   Plotinus, *Enneads* III.4.3.22.

10 For more on the henads, see Saffrey and Westerink's introduction to vol. 3 of their edition of the *Platonic Theology* (Paris, 1978), pp. ix–lxxvii.

11 *Platonic Theology* III.4 (ed. Saffrey and Westerink, pp. 14–17, and see note: pp. 112f.).

12 See, e.g., DN II.11: 649B–C; V.4: 817C.

13 See B. Brons, *Gott und die Seienden* (Göttingen, 1976), p. 194.

14 On this and what follows, see Otto Semmelroth's article, 'Gottes ausstrahlendes Licht: zur Schöpfungs- und Offenbarungslehre des Ps-Dionysius Areopagita', *Scholastik* 28 (1953), pp. 481–503: one of a series of important (but alas, somewhat inaccessible) articles on Dionysian theology.

15 DN XI.6: 953C–956A; cf. DN II.1: 636C–637C; V.2: 816C–817A.

16 See MT III: 1032D–1033A.

17 *Elements of Theology*, prop. 35.

18 See *Expositio Fidei* i.14 (ed. B. Kotter, 1973: pp. 42f.).

19 See Bernard McGinn, 'The God beyond God. Theology and mysticism in the thought of Meister Eckhart', *Journal of Religion* 61 (1981), pp. 1–19.

20 See, e.g., Origen, *On Prayer* VIII.2; Gregory of Nyssa, *On the Lord's Prayer* 1.

21 See Jean Trouillard, *L'Un et l'âme selon Proclos* (Paris, 1972), pp. 178f.

22 E. von Ivánka, 'Der Aufbau der Schrift "De divinis nominibus" des Ps-Dionysius', *Scholastik* 15 (1940), pp. 386–92; repr. in *Plato Christianus* (Einsiedeln, 1964), pp. 228–42.

23 See, especially, E. Corsini, *Il Trattato* de Divinis Nominibus *dello*

Pseudo-Dionigi e i commenti neoplatonici al Parmenide (Turin, 1962), pp. 58–73.

24   I. P. Sheldon-Williams, 'The Pseudo-Dionysius and the Holy Hierotheus', *Studia Patristica* 8 (1966), p. 114.

25   DN IV.2 does talk about *pronoia*.

26   Plato, *Laws* X.899Dff.

27   *Elements of Theology*, prop. 120.

28   On this, see Jean Trouillard, *La Mystagogie de Proclos* (Paris, 1982), pp. 101–8.

29   See Corsini, op. cit., pp. 135f.; and O. Semmelroth, 'Gottes geeinte Vielheit: zur Gotteslehre des Ps-Dionysius Areopagita', *Scholastik* 25 (1950), pp. 389–403.

30   Dodds, op. cit., p. 263.

31   See Proclus, *In Alcibiadem* 51 (ed. L. G. Westerink, Amsterdam, 1954: pp. 22f.).

32   J. Rist, 'A note on Eros and Agape in Ps-Dionysius', *Vigiliae Christianae* 20 (1966), p. 238.

33   DN XI.3–5; cf. Augustine, *The City of God* XIX.12.

6

Visions and darkness

VISIONS

In his second letter to the Corinthians, St Paul comes to talk of 'visions and revelations of the Lord' and tells of a 'man in Christ' (most probably a veiled allusion to himself) who 'was caught up to the third heaven—whether in the body or out of the body I do not know, God knows— . . . and he heard things that cannot be told, which man may not utter' (2 Cor 12:2, 4). It is not surprising then that one who wishes to be seen as a close disciple of St Paul should also speak of visions and of the ineffability of what is thus revealed, nor that he, too, tells of these visions by ascribing them to a third party. Only with Denys, the third party is no nameless 'man in Christ', but a monk, Carpus, his 'revered guide', Hierotheus, and Moses. The choice of Moses is not that surprising, either, as Moses and Paul were often bracketed together as notable recipients of the vision of God.[1]

We have already seen something of Carpus's vision which Denys describes at the end of Ep. VIII. It has a liturgical context: it took place as Carpus was praying during the night office. Another remark Denys makes about Carpus underlines the connexion he sees between visions and the liturgy: he tells us that Carpus would not celebrate the liturgy 'unless during the sacred prayers of preparation there was shown to him a favourable vision' (1097C). This may seem strange, indeed rather pagan: one recalls the story from the Sayings of the Desert Fathers:

Abba Olympios said this, 'One of the pagan priests came down to Scetis one day and came to my cell and slept there. Having reflected on the monks' way of life, he said to me, "Since you live like this, do you not receive any visions from your God?". I said to him, "No." Then the priest said to me, "Yet when we make a sacrifice to our God, he hides nothing from us, but discloses his mysteries; and you, giving yourselves so much hardship, vigils, prayer and asceticism, say that you see nothing? Truly, if you see nothing, then it is because you have wicked thoughts in your hearts, which separate you from your God, and for this reason his mysteries are not revealed to you." So I went to report the priest's words to the old men. They were filled with admiration and said that this was so. For impure thoughts separate God from man.'[2]

There is something very moving about the humility of the 'old men', conscious of their need for continual repentance and calmly unsurprised that they see no visions. But other Christians did expect to see visions, notably the author of the homilies ascribed to Macarius the Great. These homilies, of Syrian not Egyptian provenance, lay considerable stress on visions: after much struggle and prayer 'the face of the soul is unveiled, and it gazes upon the heavenly Bridegroom face to face in a spiritual light that cannot be described'.[3] This tradition was influential in Eastern monasticism and reached its apogee in Hesychasm with its doctrine of the vision of the uncreated light of God.[4] In the tenth/eleventh century, a similar emphasis on the vision of the divine light is found in Symeon the New Theologian, who regarded experience of the divine vision as a prerequisite for ecclesiastical office:[5] a generalized version of what Denys admired so much in Carpus.

DARKNESS

The short treatise, the *Mystical Theology*, seems to be about a different kind of vision. There Denys talks of Moses in his ascent of Mount Sinai. As he ascends, he passes beyond all that can be discerned by the senses and the intellect and enters into a divine darkness where he is united with God in a way that surpasses knowledge. Denys's account of the ascent of Moses into the Divine Darkness has many parallels with Gregory of Nyssa's much more extended treatment in the second part of his *Life of Moses*, and it

seems certain that Denys has drawn on it.[6] This suggests an arche-
typal 'mystical ascent', in which the soul passes beyond images and
comes to know God as he is in himself: the *Mystical Theology* was
read in that way in the Middle Ages, notably by the author of the
Cloud of Unknowing, and is still so read today. According to this
interpretation, Denys is speaking of a contemplative union with
God, where the soul abandons forms of prayer that rely on imagery
and reasoning ('meditation' as it was, and still is, called) and learns
an openness to God himself in the darkness of the abandonment of
techniques within its control. But it has been noted[7] that Denys's
account of the ascent of Mount Sinai by Moses is full of liturgical
echoes. Moses purifies himself and then, separating himself from the
crowd, ascends the mountain with his chosen priests: just as the
hierarch is purified and then approaches the altar with his priests.[8]
In his ascent he passes beyond 'all divine lights and sounds and
heavenly words' into the 'Darkness': just as the liturgy progresses
from the first part full of readings from Scripture and sacred hymns,
into the hidden (and perhaps also silent) consecration in the sanctuary. It is to be noted, too, that the *Mystical Theology* is addressed
to Timothy, a hierarch. Several times in the *Ecclesiastical Hierarchy*
the hierarch's experience of the liturgy is spoken of in terms that
recall the language of the *Mystical Theology* (especially I.3, which
describes the ascent of Moses). At the end of the rite of illumination
(or baptism) the hierarch is said to turn 'from the procession to the
secondary things and reach up to contemplation of those that are
first';[9] at the end of his account of the Eucharist, Denys says that
'while the many are content to behold the divine symbols alone, the
hierarch is ever being raised up hierarchically by the thearchic Spirit
to the holy sources of the sacramental rites in blessed and conceptual
visions, in the purity of his godlike condition' (EH III.ii: 428A); in
the case of the still more hidden sacrament of oil, the actual ceremony is said to be hidden from the ordinary people and sacredly
veiled by the priests who are allowed to behold, 'for the ray of all-
holy things enlightens purely and directly godly men, as kin of the
Light, and the fragrance is received by their minds without any hin-
drance' (EH IV.iii.2: 476B). All this suggests that the *Mystical
Theology* has a liturgical context, and indeed that it relates especially
to the hierarch and his role in the liturgy.

HIEROTHEUS AGAIN

The other visionary Denys speaks of is his guide, Hierotheus. He speaks of his 'many and blessed visions' as being the source of his teaching (DN II.9); and in DN III.2 describes the extraordinary experience Hierotheus had on the occasion of the death of Mary, the Mother of God (her 'dormition' or falling asleep) when, in the context of that solemn occasion, he surpassed the other apostles and holy men in singing praises of the 'boundlessly powerful goodness of the thearchic weakness', and being 'wholly caught up, wholly out of himself, and suffering communion with the things praised, so that he was considered by all who heard and saw him, and knew or rather did not know him, to be divinely possessed, to be uttering divine praises' (681D–684A).[10] We encounter here themes we are already familiar with: Hierotheus's ecstasy ('wholly out of himself') and his experiencing (or rather suffering) divine things. We hear, too, language that Denys characteristically uses of the liturgy: for the hierarch in the celebration of the Eucharist is said to 'come into communion' with the 'things praised' (EH III.ii: 425D).

We suggested earlier (pp. 28–29) that Hierotheus's significance is to be seen in relation to the liturgy. Now is the time to draw out what Denys says about Hierotheus, for it seems that it is Hierotheus's experience that will be our surest guide to the meaning of the *Mystical Theology*. Hierotheus's significance for Denys is spelled out in the *Divine Names*: in the two passages just referred to, and in the discussion of love (*erōs* and *agapē*) in DN IV.10ff., which culminates in extracts from Hierotheus's *Hymns of Love* (DN IV.15–17).

From all this a remarkably consistent picture emerges. Hierotheus's knowledge of the divine is derived partly from his study of the Scriptures, and partly through an untaught experience, where he did not 'learn' but 'suffered' or experienced divine things. As a result Denys speaks of his 'sympathy' with divine things, which was both an expression of and a means towards his 'hidden union and faith' (DN II.9). This sympathy, or suffering of divine things, is presented as divine possession, which issues in ecstasy. Given this language of possession, ecstasy, suffering, it is no surprise that all this is summed up in Denys's teaching on love. Love, we have seen, is defined as a 'power that unites and binds together and effects an indissoluble fusion in the beautiful and the good' (DN IV.12: 709C), and it is ecstatic in the sense that it draws the lover out of himself and centres his life on the beloved: 'those who are possessed by this love belong not to themselves, but to the objects of their love' (712A).

Denys's example of such ecstatic love of God is the apostle, St Paul, the common master of himself and Hierotheus (and of Timothy[11]):

> So also the great Paul, caught up in rapture by divine love and participating in its ecstatic power, said with inspired speech, 'I live, and yet not I, but Christ lives in me.' As a true lover, caught up out of himself into God, he lives not his own life, but that life so much longed for, the life of his beloved (DN IV.13: 712A).

Ecstasy, for Denys, does not primarily mean an extraordinary experience, it means having one's life centred on the beloved so that the life of the beloved is one's own. In the case of the love of God, it means letting God's love be the principle of one's life. It is 'suffering' in that it means receptivity of such a high degree that the one who loves God is a vehicle of his power and love. It is ecstatic in the sense that the self of the lover is driven out by the love of God. In one place, Denys speaks of the soul not so much going out of itself, as being driven out of itself (the soul is the object of the verb, *existēmi*: 'going out' or 'standing out')—and indeed being driven out of itself by the way of negation (DN XIII.3: 981B). For it is the way of negation, apophatic theology, that surrenders the soul to the unknowable God. This is precisely the teaching of the *Mystical Theology*: as Moses ascends the mount, he passes beyond what can be affirmed, and can only express what he experiences by means of negation—'now, belonging wholly to that which is beyond all, and no longer to anything, whether himself or another, and united in his highest part with him who is unknown by renunciation of all knowing, by that very not knowing he knows in a manner that transcends understanding' (MT I.3: 1001A).

To complete the picture of Hierotheus and his importance for Denys, we must look at the examples of his teaching that Denys gives: from the *Elements of Theology* and especially the *Hymns of Love*. The overriding theme here is God's love for mankind: a love that goes out from God and draws men back to himself. The circle of existence is the movement of love's procession (manifest as providential care), love's capacity to bind together equals in communion, and the returning movement of love whereby the lower strives upwards towards the higher (DN IV.15). But this movement of God towards his creation in love is not only manifest in his creative activity, providential care and the attractive allure of his beauty. It is manifest, too, in the incarnation:

Therefore out of his love for mankind [his *philanthrōpia*, the usual word in the Greek Fathers and the Greek Liturgy for God's love for mankind] he has come as far as our nature, and truly become a being, and the transcendent God is called a man. (DN II.10: 648D—from the *Elements of Theology*)

It is just these two themes—that of procession and return, and that of the incarnation—that govern Denys's understanding of the liturgy: the movement of the liturgy, especially the movement of the hierarch out among the people and back again during the censing procession, reflects the fundamental movements of procession and return, and the function of the liturgy is to celebrate the *theourgiai*, the divine acts, pre-eminently the divine activity of the incarnation (see above, pp. 73–74).

A CELEBRANT'S HANDBOOK?

The *Mystical Theology*, then, is to be seen as relating to the liturgy, as referring to the inner nature of what is accomplished in the liturgy: union with God and deification. But for *whom* does it elucidate this inner meaning? Much of what we have said so far would suggest that it is concerned with the hierarch, or bishop. It is addressed to Timothy, a hierarch. Hierotheus seems to be the model of the experience it speaks of, and he too was most likely a hierarch. Other considerations might suggest this as well. The *Mystical Theology* is speaking of what happens beyond the symbols of the liturgy and beyond the affirmations, both metaphorical and conceptual, of our praise of God. It is the theology of silence and union with God. How does the notion of such union with God relate to the hierarchies that figure so large in his books on the heavenly and earthly hierarchies? Hierarchies seem to trace a movement away from God.

The most natural suggestion (which Denys himself takes up, when he speaks of the seraphim in CH VII and VIII, and EH IV) is that union with God is the prerogative of those beings immediately present to God: the seraphim, or perhaps the whole of the first rank of angelic beings—seraphim, cherubim and thrones—who several times are said to dwell in the 'antechamber' of the Thearchy (*pro-thyroi*, a Neoplatonic expression: e.g., CH VII.2, and cf. DN V.5). Indeed, when in CH XIII Denys expands on the role of the seraphim, much of his language is reminiscent of the *Mystical Theology*.[12] Perhaps, then, in the case of our hierarchy, union with God is reserved for those who occupy the highest rank, namely the hierarchs or bishops. Much of what we have seen in this chapter suggests such an inference. Denys does seem to imply that the hierarch lives in contact with the realities that he displays in symbolic fashion for the sake of the people in the liturgy. The *Mystical Theology* would then be intended for bishops: it would be a kind of celebrant's handbook.

That may be so, but there are considerations that weigh against such a conclusion. What about the monks?—we might wonder. Their vocation is to live out a union with the One, and to draw everything into that unity. One might observe, too, that the first four of Denys's letters which seem to be appendices to the *Mystical Theology*—the first two are concerned with the notion of the divine darkness and of the divine transcendence, the central notion of the *Mystical Theology*, the other two with the meaning of the incarnation, which we have seen to be equally central—are all addressed to a *monk*, Gaius. That would suggest that Denys does not reserve the theme of the *Mystical Theology* for the attention of bishops alone. Perhaps then we should see the *two* human hierarchies—the priestly hierarchy and the lay hierarchy—as united with God through their highest rank, bishops and monks respectively?

HIERARCHY AND THE WAY OF NEGATION

But either of these suggestions implies that, in some way, the hierarchies are to be seen as ladders leading up to union with God: those at the top of the ladder are in union with God (or in reach of such union), which is denied to those lower down the hierarchy. It is certainly true that we can find examples of such an understanding of hierarchy later on in the tradition inspired by Denys, but I do not think there is much trace of it in his own writings (the most evident trace is, it seems to me, that the subject of seraphim readily invites the topic of immediate union with God). It would mean that hierarchies do not simply mediate the light of God's revelation; it would mean that they express a notion of distance from God as well. Denys rarely mentions that side of the notion of hierarchy. For him, the purpose of hierarchy is simply 'assimilation with God and union with him, as far as possible' (CH III.2: 165A). His hierarchies are *static*: they are not ladders up which one climbs, so that finally by reaching the rank of seraphim (or bishop, or monk) one attains union with God. The hierarchies seem to mediate union with God and deification by their *existence*, not by their finally being folded up as one reaches the top. The hierarchies are a glittering display of the divine glory, a magnificient *theophany*, and by responding to that theophany we are assimilated to God and deified.

In fact the *Mystical Theology* nowhere mentions the hierarchies. Perhaps, then, the hierarchies are irrelevant for the purpose of that treatise. According to the *Mystical Theology*, as one passes beyond symbols and concepts, one comes into the presence of God, a presence which seems like absence because one has passed beyond one's powers to perceive and understand. When we were discussing Denys's notion of hierarchy and its Neoplatonic background, we noticed that Denys deserts Neoplatonism in one crucial respect: the hierarchies only mediate the light of divine revelation, they do not, as Neoplatonic hierarchies do, mediate *being*. We may be illuminated by attention to those beings higher than us, but we are created, each of us, directly by God (see above, pp. 84–87). Perhaps Denys's departure from orthodox Neoplatonism is relevant here. If the hierarchies mediate *everything* we receive from the Source of all—being, life, intelligence—then to ascend to the One is to recapitulate the procession *through* the hierarchies. If, however, we are created immediately by God, and it is only the light of revelation we receive through the hierarchies, then we can be united to God by responding immediately to his act of creation. God's creative act is seen by Denys as an act of his ecstatic love: God goes out of himself, while remaining himself, in love in the act of creation. Going beyond symbols and concepts is interpreted by Denys in MT I as an act of love in which we abandon the *signs* of God's love—the symbols and concepts that reveal him and his love—and come to belong to God himself, for love has the effect of taking us out of ourselves and surrendering us to the Beloved. The way of negation, apophatic theology, is then the way of ecstatic love, answering God's ecstatic love for his creatures. It realizes an immediate relationship with God.

This comes out still more clearly if we consider what is involved in Denys's understanding of the way of negation. For the way of negation is only partly something that we *do*: in MT II he draws on a famous metaphor Plotinus used[13] when he says:

> For this is to see and to know truly, and to praise in a transcendent way him who is beyond being through the negation of all things, just as those who make statues with their own hands cut away everything which obscures the clear beholding of the

hidden form, and thus make it manifest its hidden beauty solely by the process of cutting away. (MT II: 1025B)

suffer But more importantly, it is something that we *suffer*, something that happens to us. So Denys speaks of the soul in deep darkness being united with the One who is unknown by 'inactivity (*anenergēsia*) of knowing' (MT I.3: 1001A), by a passivity of the intellect. Elsewhere he says, as we have seen (p. 103), that the ascent through negation prises the soul out of itself, the ecstasy happening to the soul as an object.[14] Perhaps one should make a separation between 'negative theology' and 'mystical theology': negative theology remaining a matter of human understanding, while mystical theology is a matter of surrender to the dark ray of divine light, a matter of a 'theopathic state', as it has been called.[15] But that would be a conceptual distinction only: the two theologies are correlative, and Denys never separates them. But mystical theology as a passive state of loving surrender to God is the deepest meaning of that 'suffering divine things' which, for Denys, was the heart of Hierotheus's experience and of his authenticity and authority as a guide in divine things. And it involves an immediate relationship, a contact, with God.

Another way of understanding the immediacy of the creature's relationship to God, which is fulfilled in union with God and seems to bypass the notion of the hierarchies, and the distance from God they seem to entail, is to consider Denys's notion of paradigms or predeterminations (above, p. 94), and the related notion of analogy. The creature's response to God is not to draw near to God by ascending the hierarchy, but to identify itself with God's will (another word for paradigm or predetermination) by fulfilling its role in the created order, by fulfilling the analogy between itself and the Creator that the Creator himself has determined. Praising God 'according to the analogy of all those beings of which he is the Cause' (DN VII.3: 872A) is the same thing as 'assimilation to God as far as possible'.[16] The Platonic qualification 'as far as possible' (*kata to dynaton*) has for Denys a precise meaning: it is the same as 'according to the analogy' (*kata tēn analogian*), where analogy means the aptitude of the creature to receive the divine, an aptitude given by God and perfected by the creature's co-operation with God. To perfect the analogy given by God is not to ascend the hierarchy—that would breach the God-given analogy—but to perfect one's place in the hierarchy which is determined by the analogy God has established between each unique creature and himself. The analogy of each creature is perfected by love (DN IV.5: 700C−701A), and the way of love is, we have just seen, the way of negation and surrender.[17]

If the 'ascent through negations', ultimately involving mystical theology, is to be drawn up to God and ecstatically out of oneself in an act of loving surrender, then the human ecstasy of union with God and the divine ecstasy of creation can be seen as meeting one another: God goes out of himself in love in establishing the creature's being, the creature goes out of itself in love in union with its Creator. And this act of mutual ecstasy bypasses the system of hierarchy: just as God bypasses the hierarchies in creation, so the creature bypasses the hierarchies in realizing its immediate relationship to God in ecstatic love. What then would be the point of the hierarchies? The only point Denys ever ascribes to them: to display the divine glory, to be limpid, diaphanous theophany, and thus to call back to God those creatures that have lost their sense of divine origin, and their sense of the divine beauty. Beauty calls everything to itself (a play on words in Greek where 'beauty' is *kallos*, and 'to call' is *kalein*[18]): the beauty and splendour of the hierarchies call out to the whole creation. But the hierarchies *are* the creation, the cosmos, and intelligent creatures, who have free choice, can enhance or mar the transmission of the divine glory through the hierarchy. Hence the emphasis Denys lays on the necessity for purity in the priestly ranks, for their role is to mediate to those lower down. But it is an emphasis that is equally appropriate to all rational beings. If this is right, then the *Mystical Theology* is not to be restricted to bishops, or even to bishops and monks: it deeply concerns them, but it concerns all who want to be faithful to the divine vision.

To say this, however, is not to say that the *Mystical Theology* is after all a kind of erratic block in the Dionysian Corpus, in that it is not concerned with liturgical theology. Rather the point is that it concerns the heart of the liturgy, the inner 'mystic' meaning, the manifestation of God's love in divine acts that culminate in the incarnation. It is not concerned with thinking about God's love, or explaining it, but simply with experiencing it, 'suffering' it. The liturgical action is an invitation to open oneself to the divine love: to respond to that invitation is to allow the whole of one's life to be transformed, to be deified, to become a vehicle for God's love in the world. The liturgical invitation is addressed to human beings of body and soul: it is expressed in symbols and concepts, in liturgical actions and gestures, and hymns and prayers. To understand and respond is to enter into the meaning of these ceremonies, which is God's *philan-*

108

thrōpia, his love for all humanity. And that response is required of all who take part in the liturgy. As he explains each sacred rite, Denys passes from the 'mystery' to 'contemplation' (*theōria*): and all the baptized are expected to contemplate, to watch, to take part, to be involved in the movement of God's love. It is the rank of the holy people whom Denys calls the 'contemplative order'.

Notes

1 E.g., Gregory of Nyssa expounds Moses' vision by reference to Paul's in the *Life of Moses* II.173ff. ; and for Augustine on the visions of Moses and Paul, see C. Butler, *Western Mysticism* (2nd ed., London, 1926), pp. 78–88.

2 Alphabetical Collection, Olympios, 1 (PG 65: 313C–D), trans. (with modifications) by Benedicta Ward SLG, *The Sayings of the Desert Fathers* (London, 1975), p. 135.

3 Macarius, *Homily* X.4 (trans. A. J. Mason, London, 1921; p. 78).

4 See Vladimir Lossky, *The Mystical Theology of the Eastern Church* (Eng. trans., Cambridge, 1957), pp. 217–35.

5 See *Ethical Treatise* V.11.404–54, and Darrouzès' remarks in his introduction: *Sources Chrétiennes* 122 (Paris, 1966), pp. 33–5.

6 See H.-C. Puech's article, 'La Ténèbre mystique chez le Pseudo-Denys l'Aréopagite', repr. in *En quête de la gnose* (Paris, 1978), pp. 119–41; esp. pp. 131f.

7 Notably by Paul Rorem in a paper (as yet unpublished) given at the Ninth International Patristic Conference in 1983, and in his notes to the translation of MT in *Works*.

8 EH III.ii: 425C–D; cf. EH III.iii.10.

9 EH II.ii.8: 397A; cf. EH III.iii.3: 429B.

10 The translation in the *Classics of Western Spirituality* gives the impression of a *vision* of the Mother of God shared by the apostles, Hierotheus and Denys himself. The point is, surely, that they were there and saw the body of Mary.

11 See DN VII.1.

12 See, especially, CH XIII.4: 304C; the account of the seraphim in EH IV.iii.5–10 has, however, very few echoes of MT.

13 *Ennead* I.6.9.9ff.

14 DN XIII.3: 981B.

15 See Roques, *Structures*, pp. 143–5.

16 The Platonic phrase (from *Theaetetus* 176B) and the idea of analogy mutually echo each other in CH III.2: 165A–C.

17 See V. Lossky, 'La notion des "analogies" chez Denys le Pseudo-Aréopagite', *Archives d'histoire doctrinale et littéraire du moyen-âge* 5 (1931), pp. 279–309; O. Semmelroth, 'Die Lehre des Ps-Dionysius Areopagita vom Aufstieg der Kreatur zum göttlichen Licht', *Scholastik* 29 (1954), pp. 24–52.

18 An etymology that goes back to Plato: *Cratylus* 416C.

7

Afterlife

The writings ascribed to Denys the Areopagite were destined to have a long and fruitful influence. This influence was obviously enhanced by their claim to have been written by St Paul's convert and disciple, but it cannot be reduced to that: those who succumbed to their influence were not 'duped', but responded to the power of the vision they express. In this chapter we can do no more than indicate the general lines of his influence, such were its many and complex ramifications.[1] The story of his influence is, in fact, several stories: there is the story of his influence throughout the Byzantine centuries in Greek Christianity, an influence that eventually reached the Slav countries; there is the story of his influence in the Latin West, first by distant echoes in those still open to influence from the Greeks and then through the study of the various translations of the Dionysian Corpus that were made in the Middle Ages, first into Latin, and later into the various modern vernaculars. But the earliest story is the story of the influence of the Dionysian writings in that milieu that was so close to their begetting: the milieu of Syrian Christianity.

THE SYRIAN STORY

We have noticed, throughout this book, various striking parallels between Denys and Syrian Christianity: parallels that support the supposition that Denys's geographical milieu was Syria. It is not surprising then that the very first translation of the Areopagitical Corpus was into Syriac, a dialect of Aramaic that came to serve as the

literary language of the majority of Christians living in Eastern pro-
vinces of the Roman Empire and, over the frontier, in the Persian
Empire. This was made very early indeed, by Sergius of Reshaina
who died in 536: it almost certainly antedates the first occasion when
the writings of Denys are known to have been cited, at the Council at
Constantinople in 532. This translation was revised by Phocas of
Edessa in the late seventh century. Its influence (as with the Greek
tradition, see below) can be traced in two ways: through commen-
taries and scholia (brief explanatory comments), and the use of
Dionysian ideas in writers who had read him. But the Dionysian
tradition in Syrian Christianity is only one of several traditions, and
amongst those traditions the Dionysian influence is usually sub-
ordinate: there do not seem to have been any Dionysian disciples.
Apart from the native traditions of Syriac-speaking Christianity,
which has left its own mark on Denys, much monastic literature was
translated into Syriac and found a ready audience. The sayings of the
Fathers of the Desert, Palladius's *Lausiac History* and the *History of
the Monks in Egypt* were all available in Syriac probably even before
Denys wrote his own works (in the seventh century this material was
all put together to form *The Paradise of the Fathers*[2]). Various of the
Macarian Homilies were also translated into Syriac, and several
writings of Evagrius of Pontus, the great theorist of the monastic life
who died in 399 (notably his *Kephalaia Gnostica*—'Gnostic
Chapters'—which have not survived in Greek, but survive in two
Syriac translations, both probably earlier than Sergius of Reshaina's
translation of Denys[3]). So a wealth of material on the monastic life,
and the two great traditions of interpretation of that life—the
experiential Macarian tradition, and the more intellectualist, Origenist tradition of Evagrius—were available in the Syriac-speaking
world into which Denys was introduced by the Syriac translations. In
that context Denys could only be another voice, speaking of angels,
the liturgy and introducing a new kind of language for speaking
about the nearest approach to God, the language of darkness. This is
just what we find, for example, in Simeon 'the Graceful'
(*d-Taybutheh*), who lived in what is now northern Iraq in the seventh
century.[4] He acknowledges his debt to Denys the Areopagite, and
speaks of the three orders of reality—God the Trinity, the realm of
the angels, and the realm of men and women—and he has a strong
sense of divine providence 'which holds all, deifies all, perfects all,
illuminates all, and which by its perfect goodness penetrates all,
sustains all, and infuses all with the desire of uniting with the highest
Divinity',[5] and regards the highest knowledge of God as 'no-

knowledge, or rather a knowledge that is higher than all knowledge, as it has reached the divine knowledge of the hidden God, which is higher than all understanding':[6] all of which is very reminiscent of Denys. But it is all in the context of teaching which is much more markedly Evagrian: prayer is, for example, 'an emptiness of the mind and a peaceful and rational intelligence . . . a complete destruction of thoughts and a complete rejection of all cares';[7] there is emphasis on *apatheia* and a very Evagrian understanding of the soul's ascent to God. Dionysian themes are interwoven into a fundamentally Evagrian fabric. When we find in the Syrian tradition the only real attempt to continue the enterprise of Dionysian pseudonymity, it is in the service of an advanced Evagrianism which would otherwise have been short-lived. For the 'Book of Hierotheus', purporting to come from Denys's revered teacher, was written by Stephen bar Sudhaili not long after the composition of the Areopagitical Corpus itself, and though it contains many Dionysian traits, these are only to give 'authenticity' to a work that is deeply and uncompromisingly Evagrian.[8]

THE GREEK STORY

The story of Dionysian influence in the Byzantine East is not fundamentally different from the Syrian story. By the time Denys wrote, the main sources of the Byzantine tradition were already in place: the theology of the Cappadocians, and of Cyril of Alexandria, the preaching of St John Chrysostom, the monastic literature—the accounts of the Desert Fathers, both the collections of sayings, and the lives and histories—and the two strands of interpretation of the monastic life, the Macarian and the Evagrian, as well as the earliest attempts to draw these traditions into a synthesis, notably the attempt of Diadochus of Photike. The Dionysian literature introduces another voice, a voice that speaks in a strange accent, at once too Syrian and too Greek: too close to the monks who mistrusted Chalcedon, and too close to the 'Hellenes', the representatives of the pagan Greek philosophical tradition. The earliest evidence of Dionysian influence is found in scholia on his writings. These were long ascribed to Maximus the Confessor, who did indeed write some of them, and they are printed as his in the columns of Migne's *Patrologia Graeca* (vol. 4). But the earliest scholia, the basic collection to which others were added, were written by John of Scythopolis.[9] This John was a man of astonishing erudition: indeed his erudition may have included knowledge of the real author of the Areopagitical writings. Certainly he was very close to their inspiration, and his scholia shed light on the philosophical filiation of the Dionysian ideas.[10] Much of his effort in the scholia was to save Denys for the adherents of Chalcedon: Denys's ambiguities were read in a way contrary to that of the Monophysites who cited him in 532, by which time John's scholia were already written. So though Denys remained popular amongst those who opposed Chalcedon, he was still able to find favour amongst those who supported Chalcedon. Leontius of Jerusalem (sixth century) cites him, as does the author of *De Sectis* (once ascribed to the other sixth-century Leontius, of Byzantium).

But the most important person to be influenced by Denys, and the one who decisively secured his acceptance by the Orthodox, was St Maximus the Confessor (580–662). Maximus was involved in the last stages of the Christological controversy, the beginnings of which we have already traced. Now the controversy was over the human will of Christ. There were those who denied that Christ had a human will and believed that he had only a single (divine) will: their opponents called them Monotheletes (from the Greek for a 'single will'). Their position seemed a good compromise which might serve to secure the reconciliation of the Monophysites, and enable Byzantine Christianity to present a united front against the new threat of Islam. In the space of three years (638–641), Arab troops had overrun the whole area from the Arabian Desert to the Sahara, and within only a few years more Syria was to become the hub of a Muslim empire greater than that of Rome at its height. The pressure to conform to the Monothelete position was enormous and Maximus's continued opposition to the heresy led to his condemnation in 662. After being flogged and mutilated, he died in August of that year, an exile in the Caucasus. Maximus was soon vindicated—at the Sixth Ecumenical Council held in 680–681 in Constantinople—and held in veneration as 'the Confessor'. His theological achievement is a work of synthesis drawing together Cappadocian and Cyrilline theology, Macarian experiential spirituality, the psychological and philosophical insights of Evagrius . . . and the vision, both theological and philosophical, of Denys the Areopagite. He also, as we have seen, wrote scholia on the Dionysian writings, but his real importance lies in the way he found a place for Dionysian ideas and Dionysian language in a synthesis drawing on all the resources of Byzantine theology and spirituality. The basis of the synthesis is not Denys: on the theological side his main authority is Cyrilline Christology and the ideas of the Cappadocians, on the side of spirituality a synthesis of Macarius and Evagrius. The impact of Denys is mainly felt in deepening the apophatic stress of Cappadocian theology—Denys's language of transcendent attributes of God (prefaced by *hyper-*) is welcomed, as is also his language of 'apophatic' and 'cataphatic' theology—an endorsement of his understanding of the ranks of heavenly beings (though not the subordination of the historical incarnate Jesus to them), and, in the realm of spirituality, the grafting on to the Macarian–Evagrian synthesis of the triad, purification–illumination–perfection (which is also applied to the apostolic ministry in a Dionysian way), and the idea that in the final stages of its ascent to God, the soul advances into a realm of unknowing and knows God in an ecstasy of love. In two other ways the influence of Denys is perhaps more profound. What attracted Denys to Neoplatonism, we have surmised, was the subtle understanding of reality he found there. To a certain extent, the same is true of Denys's attraction for Maximus: the analysis of reality that we find in Denys (of largely Neoplatonic inspiration) impressed Maximus in turn. For though Maximus rarely uses Denys's Neoplatonic language of procession and return, speaking instead of God's movement towards us in incarnation and self-emptying and our movement of return and response as deification and renunciation, and understanding God's relation to creation as fundamentally and explicitly one of creation out of nothing, Maximus makes much use of the fundamental triads of being–power–activity, being–life–intelligence, and (perhaps most fundamentally) being–well being–eternal being, all of which can be traced back to the Neoplatonic analysis of reality we find in Denys.

The other way in which Denys's influence is deeply felt is in his *Mystagōgia*, his introduction to the liturgy of the Church. This is often misunderstood (as is Denys's *Ecclesiastical Hierarchy*) as foreshadowing the elaborately allegorical interpretations of the ceremonies of the liturgy found in the Western Middle Ages.[11] But Maximus (and Denys) is far from the arbitrary individualism of such interpretation. He sees the Eucharist as the action of the whole Church, and has a sense of the dramatic structure of the rite as a unity: all of which he derives from Denys. He goes beyond Denys in making more of the spatial aspect of the liturgy, and in his grasp of its eschatological significance. The first part of the *Mystagōgia* concerns the symbolism of the Church building, which in its unity in diversity is an image of God, and, in the division of the Church building into the sanctuary (*hierateion*) and the nave (*naos*), reflects similar divisions in the cosmos (between the invisible and the visible orders), the physical world (heaven and earth), man (body and soul), soul (contemplative intellect and practical reason), Scripture (mystical and literal meaning). The movement of the liturgy between sanctuary and nave can therefore be seen to echo at all levels from the cosmic to the individual.

Maximus was deeply influential on the tradition of Byzantine theology: a measure of his importance for the later monastic tradition in the East can be seen in the fact that he is assigned more space than anyone else in the *Philokalia* of St Nicodemus of the Holy Mountain and St Macarius of Corinth (163 pages out of 1,206 in the *editio princeps* of 1782; most of the second volume of the English translation). The influence of Denys on St Maximus was therefore widely felt throughout the Byzantine East. Nevertheless there are still Byzantine writers totally unaffected by Denys: notably St John Climacus, a close contemporary of Maximus, whose *Ladder of Divine Ascent* is perhaps as important in Eastern Orthodox monasticism as the Rule of St Benedict in the West. But from the time of Maximus onwards, Dionysian themes become more and more commonly accepted. In the century after Maximus, the influence of Denys can be traced along lines by now familiar in the works of St John Damascene (*c.* 650–*c.* 750). John follows Denys for his angelology, and takes over his language of apophatic and cataphatic theology, and other aspects of Denys's doctrine of the divine names (for example, in relation to the doctrines of the Trinity and the incarnation), but this is all part of a much wider synthesis that owes most to others—others with whom we are already familiar.

If John Damascene represents Dionysian influence in the wake of Maximus on the theological side, then Germanus of Constantinople (who died in 733 and was the Damascene's contemporary and with him one of the principal opponents of iconoclasm) can be taken as representing that influence on the liturgical side. His 'Ecclesiastical History and Mystical Contemplation' (to translate it literally: a more idiomatic translation would be, 'What takes place in Church and its hidden meaning') gives an account of the Eucharistic liturgy and its significance that leans heavily on Denys's *Ecclesiastical Hierarchy*, as well as incorporating the typological understanding of the liturgy characteristic of Theodore of Mopsuestia's Homilies, and notable by its absence from Denys. The very first chapter epitomizes this double filiation: 'The Church is an earthly heaven in which God, who is beyond the heavens, dwells, and which represents the crucifixion, burial and resurrection of Christ'.[12] Germanus's interpretation of the liturgy remained dominant in Constantinople for the rest of the Byzantine period: it was unchallenged until Nicolas Cabasilas's commentary on the Divine Liturgy in the fourteenth century.[13] Through it the influence of Denys remained powerfully felt.

In the eleventh century there is a curious example of Dionysian influence in the disciple and biographer of St Symeon the New Theologian, Nicetas Stethatos (c. 1005–c. 1080). In Symeon himself Dionysian echoes are rare: he occasionally refers to the Divine Darkness,[14] but for the most part he breathes quite a different atmosphere, that of the Macarian Homilies and the felt vision of divine light. But the third section of Nicetas's trilogy, entitled 'On the Hierarchies' (the other two parts being 'On the Soul' and 'On Paradise'),[15] is both indebted to Denys and attempts to take his ideas on the hierarchies further. The concern of this treatise is to relate the two hierarchies, the celestial and the ecclesiastical. He does this by seeing the celestial hierarchy as the destiny of the ecclesiastical hierarchy: after death the faithful members of the ecclesiastical hierarchy find their allotted place amongst the ranks of the celestial hierarchy. We noticed Denys's unusual agnosticism about the afterlife (its details, that is, not the hope of the resurrection itself); Nicetas Stethatos clearly felt there was a gap here to be filled.

This theme is introduced in three successive chapters. We are told that the rank of the thrones, cherubim and seraphim (in apparently *descending* order: Nicetas reverses the Dionysian order) is the place of rest for apostles and prophets, and 'the holy God-bearing Fathers and universal teachers': those, that is, who have ascended 'from natural contemplation to mystical theology', and have 'brought forth fruit a hundred-fold', offering to the Church the 'grape of the word of wisdom in theology' (17). Nicetas characterizes the qualifications for this, the loftiest place of reponse, in three ways. First, he thinks of the most venerable members of the Church: apostles, prophets, fathers and teachers (there is still an echo here of St Paul's 'apostles, prophets, evangelists, pastors and teachers' of Eph 4:11). Secondly, they have reached the highest level in their ascent to God, which Nicetas calls by the Dionysian term 'mystical theology': here the Dionysian term simply expands the Evagrian *theologia*, for it is the Evagrian triad, *praktikē* –*physikē* (i.e., natural contemplation)–*theologia*, that he has in mind, as the sequel makes clear. (Elsewhere, Nicetas modifies the Dionysian triad, purification–illumination–perfection, into purificatory–illuminative–mystical.[16]) Thirdly, Nicetas is applying to all this the threefold fruitfulness of the seeds that fell on good ground in the parable of the Sower (Mk 4:3–20 and parallels): these bear the heaviest fruit, a hundred-fold. The rank of the dominions, powers and authorities is the place of rest for the martyrs and confessors and the holy ascetics who work miracles: these have ascended from practical philosophy to the heights of contemplation, they bear fruit a moderate sixty-fold, and offer to the Church the seed of the word of knowledge (18). The rank of the principalities, archangels and angels is the place of rest for leaders and holy abbots and lay people of holy life: these have fulfilled the commandments and have shown themselves accomplished in practical philosophy, they bear fruit thirty-fold and offer within the Church protection and relief for the needy (19).

That is Nicetas's first attempt at relating the two hierarchies: in the succeeding chapters he offers a more detailed account, which attempts a more precise correlation of the several ranks. To do this he produces three ranks of three in the ecclesiastical hierarchy to match more exactly the celestial hierarchy. Denys, we recall, had only two ranks of members of the Church: the clerical and the lay. In comparison, Nicetas's ecclesiastical hierarchy is thoroughly clerical. His highest rank consists of patriarchs, metropolitans and archbishops; his middle rank is Denys's clerical hierarchy (called by their usual names: bishops, priests—as in Denys, but now the usual ecclesiastical term—and deacons); and his lowest rank consists of sub-deacons, lectors and monks (some manuscripts bracket the lectors and monks together, thus making room for the laity as the lowest rank: but this seems to be a later modification). There is a direct correspondence between the two hierarchies: thrones correspond to patriarchs, cherubim to metropolitans, seraphim to archbishops, and so on. Each triadic rank is said to have its own chant or hymn of praise. Nicetas works out appropriate chants with some ingenuity. The thrones, etc. sing 'Blessed be the glory of the Lord in his place' (Ezek 3:12); the patriarchs, etc. sing 'Blessed be the kingdom of the Father and the Son and the Holy Spirit, now and for ever, and to the ages of ages' (the introductory chant of the Eucharistic liturgy, sung by the celebrant). The dominions, etc. sing the *sanctus* in the version as it appears in Isaiah, 'Holy, holy, holy is the Lord of Sabaoth: the whole earth is full of his glory' (Isa 6:3—oddly enough, said in Isaiah to be the song of the *seraphim*); the bishops, etc. sing the *sanctus* in its liturgical form, 'Holy, holy, holy, Lord of Sabaoth: heaven and earth are full of thy glory; hosanna in the highest. Blessed is he who comes in the name of the Lord; hosanna in the highest.' The lowest rank, both in heaven and on earth, sing simply, 'Alleluia! Alleluia! Alleluia!' After death, the members of the earthly hierarchy pass to their corresponding place in the celestial hierarchy and join the heavenly members of that hierarchy in singing their songs, thus 'forming a choir together with them and making festival with them in joy and delight' (56). In this parallelism, Nicetas displays his deep sense of the earthly liturgy as an anticipation of the heavenly liturgy. One recalls the impression made on the envoys of Vladimir, Prince of Kiev, by the liturgy in the Church of the Holy Wisdom at Constantinople, only a few decades before Nicetas wrote, according to the account in the *Russian Primary Chronicle*: 'We knew not whether we were in heaven or on earth, for surely there is no such splendour or beauty anywhere on earth'. Nicetas then continues by going through each rank, both of angels and men, pointing out the appropriateness of the place of each in its hierarchy.

He breaks off this exercise, however, with the consideration: what if 'the radiant wisdom of God the Word and the heavenly knowledge' is seen 'as light' by priests, inferior ministers and monks, but to a lesser degree, or even not at all, by bishops? (32) This doubt is an echo of the famously controversial opinion of his master, St Symeon the New Theologian, that only those who are granted the vision of divine light can really exercise the priesthood: a point we have already noticed, as it seems to be the position of the Areopagite too. Nicetas's answer is uncompromisingly on the side of Symeon (and Denys): only ordination by the Spirit counts, human ordination is no more than recognition of spiritual attainment (36: though Nicetas supports his opinion with texts that seem hardly appropriate—1 Tim 4:14 and Acts 19:6).

As Nicetas works his way through the ranks of the angelic and human beings, much of what he says is drawn from Denys. A few points are worth noticing. It seems that he reverses the order of the highest rank of angelic beings in order to place the thrones in immediate proximity to God, because they are 'receptive of the thearchic manifestation and god-bearing' (25: as Denys says, cf. CH VII.1: 205D). He parallels lectors and archangels, because they both have the role of interpreting (51f.), and monks and angels, not only because it had been customary for centuries to refer to the monastic state as the 'angelic life', but because the monks 'lead those of pagan origin to the knowledge of God', a reference presumably to the idea expounded in Denys that the angels have care of the nations, and also perhaps to the part played by the monks in the Christianization of the Slav nations, which was contemporary with Nicetas.[17]

Nicetas's development of Dionysian ideas is unusually detailed and not altogether attractive: his clericalism exceeds even that of Denys. But it gives a glimpse of continued interest in Dionysian ideas in the eleventh century. The language and ideas of the Areopagite continued to be important in Byzantine Christianity. The controversy between St Gregory Palamas and Barlaam the Calabrian is now seen by some scholars as less a conflict between Western influences (represented by Barlaam) and authentic Orthodox spirituality, as a conflict within Greek Christianity about the true meaning of Dionysian language about the knowledge of God: Barlaam interpreting his apophatic theology as intellectual dialectic, and Gregory seeing it as concerned with ineffable experience of God.[18] If Gregory represents the continued influence of Denys in his understanding of a loving encounter with God in the divine darkness, then his contemporary and supporter, Nicolas Cabasilas, represents the continued influence of Denys's liturgical theology. In his *Commentary on the Divine Liturgy*[19] and his *Life in Christ*,[20] there are marked Dionysian traces: notably, in the latter, in the way he classifies the Christian sacraments as a triad of baptism, the Eucharist, and the sacrament of chrism.

The Dionysian influence in Byzantine theology has been much deplored by modern Orthodox, and also minimized.[21] What this survey brings out is that the Dionysian strand is but one strand in the rich fabric of Byzantine theology and spirituality, and that it is the whole of the Dionysian tradition—its understanding of apophatic and cataphatic theology, its angelology and sense of the structure and nature of the Church, in fact its character as a *liturgical theology*—that has continued to inform Byzantine and Orthodox theology. The picture in the West, as we shall see, has been somewhat different.

THE LATIN STORY[22]

The first notice of Denys the Areopagite in the West comes from Pope Gregory the Great, who probably brought a codex of the Areopagitical Corpus back with him on his return from his mission as papal legate to the Emperor in Constantinople (*c*. 585). Gregory's knowledge of Greek is a subject over which there is scholarly dispute, but it was hardly likely to have been adequate for him to cope with the rather difficult Greek of the Areopagite. Nonetheless he does refer to Denys and had gained some idea of what he wrote.

But probably not very much. In Homily 34 on the Gospels, he mentions Denys's opinion that amongst the angels some are devoted to the worship of God and others minister to human needs. He rejects it on the grounds that it was one of the seraphim, the most exalted of the angelic beings, who had ministered to the prophet Isaiah. But he does not show any awareness of Denys's lengthy discussion of this very point (in CH XIII) which suggests he did not know of it. Nor is there any reason to read much significance into the fact that in that same homily he records his own view that there are nine ranks of heavenly beings. His account of the angelic ranks is not that of Denys. His order is different—seraphim, cherubim, thrones, dominions, principalities, authorities, powers, archangels, angels: this order was to remain canonical in the West until the twelfth century, when it was supplanted by the Dionysian order. Nor does he seem to think—and this is the distinctive point about the Dionysian ordering—that they are arranged in three ranks of three. As we have seen, nine ranks of angels with the names Denys gives them is an easy deduction from the biblical evidence, and can be found in the Christian tradition independently of Denys, and indeed earlier than him. As Gregory seems unaware of the distinctively Dionysian point of the three triads, there seems little reason to suppose that he knew anything much about Dionysian angelology at all, still less that he was influenced by it (he rejects the only opinion of Denys's that he mentions).

After Gregory the Great there are a few references to Denys in seventh-century documents, but the real beginning of his influence in the West came with the gift of a codex of the Dionysian writings sent by the Byzantine Emperor Michael the Stammerer to Louis the Pious in 827. This Louis gave to the monastery of Saint-Denis, north of Paris, and there the abbot, Hilduin, made a translation so bad as to be unintelligible. It was probably Hilduin who added the final embellishment to the Dionysian legend by identifying the Areopagite, the author of the Dionysian writings, with the martyr-bishop of Paris. Very soon, however, Charles the Bald commissioned another translation of Denys's works from the Irish monk, John the Scot (that is, the Irishman), or Eriugena, as he called himself. (The name *Eriugena* means native of Erin, i.e. Ireland, probably coined after the analogy of the Vergilian *Graiugena*.)

Eriugena's translation of Denys was part of a considerable work of translation which made available in the West some of the most important works of Greek theology. Apart from translating the *Corpus Areopagiticum*, he translated Gregory of Nyssa's *On the*

Creation of Man (which he called *De Imagine*) and Maximus the Confessor's *Ambigua* and *Questions to Thalassius* (these are all that has survived: it is likely that he translated other Greek works, including some by Basil and Epiphanius). These were translated (and his translation of the Dionysian writings also revised) during the 860s. At the same time he was engaged on his own work *Periphyseon* ('On nature'), in which the influence of Dionysian Neoplatonism is manifest, and his commentary on Denys's *Celestial Hierarchy*. In the 870s he began a commentary on the Fourth Gospel, of which some portions survive, and wrote a long homily on the Johannine prologue: these works bear the mark of his learning in Greek theology, and are full of Dionysian themes. Eriugena's work created a rare window through which the Latin West could look and see something of the genius of Greek theology, and at the centre of that picture was the figure of Denys the Areopagite. His own work developed Dionysian themes and gave them some currency in the West. Particularly central to Eriugena's own vision was the Dionysian idea of the world as a theophany, as a manifestation of the splendour of the divine glory, and the idea that this theophany—in the ordered cosmos, and in the incarnation—calls on man to share God's nature, to be deified.

But the work of Eriugena did not immediately awaken an echo in the West: it seems to have been neglected for two centuries. Neither Lanfranc (*c.* 1010–89) nor Anselm (*c.* 1033–1109) seems to know of it, though Suger, abbot of Saint-Denis from 1122 to 1151, drew on Dionysian themes to explain how the architecture of his new 'Gothic' abbey church helped raise the soul to God.[23] The influence of Eriugena—his works and his translations—seems first to have been felt in the Cathedral schools of the eleventh century, especially at Laon. Anselm of Laon (d. 1117) promoted Eriugena's reputation and in the *Glossa Ordinaria*, a vast collection of comments on Scripture, in the making of which he played a great part, he drew heavily on Eriugena's writings and his translations of the Areopagite. It was through the *Glossa Ordinaria* that Denys first began to exercise any influence in the West. Another translation of Denys was made, by John Saracen, a friend of John of Salisbury and at his suggestion: this and Eriugena's translation, his commentary on the *Celestial Hierarchy* and his own *Periphyseon* formed the basis for the study of philosophy in the university of Paris in the thirteenth century.[24] Another translation of part of the Dionysian corpus (DN and MT) was made by Robert Grosseteste in the thirteenth century.

It seems that Denys made his influence felt through the Schools: he was not very influential in the revival of monasticism in the twelfth century. Isaac of Stella (mid-twelfth century) seems to have known him well, but the great Cistercian reformer, St Bernard of Clairvaux, seems to have been little influenced by him.[25] The eventual influence of Denys in the West cannot, however, be understood without a grasp of Bernard's impact on Western spirituality. In Bernard we begin to see a disjunction between knowledge and love, thinking and feeling, that was destined to have a profound influence in the West.[26] In earlier thinkers (Augustine, for instance) feeling and thinking are held together, so that in love, the intellect realizes a deeper dimension of its own nature: in love, the intellect passes beyond a dispassionate discursive kind of thought, and comes to know the beloved in an intuitive way, through some kind of communion. In Bernard, however, love is opposed to knowledge, it is a matter of feeling. Knowledge is regarded as superficial—it is only thinking about things; feeling engages the depths of the human person—it is in love that a man discovers himself.

It is this tendency to separate love and knowledge that prepares the way for the peculiar form of Dionysian influence in the West. But this separation of love and knowledge can be seen as part of a much wider phenomenon—what has been called the 'discovery of the individual'[27]—and that, too, prepared the ground for the reception of Denys.

Denys's notion of hierarchy seems to have been taken up as a major interpretative concept in the high Middle Ages. St Bonaventure, for instance, develops Denys's idea in an original way by extending the notion of hierarchy up into the divine nature itself, and down into the human soul.[28] Everything is seen as hierarchical: the notion of hierarchy is used to hold together the idea of different levels in a single whole. The several hierarchies—the divine, the heavenly, the ecclesiastical, and the psychological—all mutually illuminate one another: in particular, the heavenly hierarchy, which stretches from human contact to the presence of God himself, illuminates the psychological hierarchy which itself stretches from human concerns and efforts to surrender to God in contemplation. The soul's ascent to God is an ascent through the hierarchy of the soul: it can be compared to ascent through the ranks of the celestial hierarchy. We noticed earlier that Denys himself does not regard the hierarchies as ladders for us to ascend: but it is just such an understanding of hierarchy we find emerging here. Probably the earliest example of such an understanding of hierarchy is to be found in Thomas Gallus (d. 1246), one of the canons of Saint-Victor who later became abbot of St Andrew's at Vercelli. He was devoted to the Areopagite and his commentary on Saracen's translation of the *Mystical Theology* was destined to be very influential. Thomas interprets Denys's celestial hierarchy as being a kind of allegory of the stages of the soul's ascent to God.[29] The lowest hierarchy is the level of man's natural effort, passing from simple apprehension of good and evil (the level of the angels) to the first awakening of the intellect and the affections (archangels) to the supreme truth and goodness as such (principalities); the intermediate hierarchy is the level at which man's freewill co-operates with God's grace and man is raised from a deliberate choice of what is good and true in creatures (the level of the authorities) to the perfect activity of the will aided by ordinary grace (dominions); the highest hierarchy is the level where grace alone operates and the soul moves from reception of infused grace (the level of thrones), through the perfection of knowledge by infused illumination (cherubim), to the perfection of union in the *apex affectus*, the pinnacle of the soul's feeling (the level of the seraphim). In this way, Thomas Gallus explores the hierarchical structure of the soul, seeing in it a reflection of the celestial hierarchy. We have thus an *interiorization* of the celestial hierarchy: the notion of hierarchy is being used to explore the inner depths of the individual. In this way we can see how Dionysian notions (in a very un-Dionysian context) contributed to the 'discovery of the individual'.

Very much the same picture is found in Bonaventure's popular *Journey of the Soul into God* (and it is most likely that Bonaventure was influenced by Thomas Gallus):

These things attained, our spirit, inasmuch as it is in conformity with the heavenly Jerusalem, is made hierarchic in order to mount upwards . . . Thus our spirit is sealed with the nine degrees of orders, when in its inner depths the following are arranged in due order: announcing, dictating, guiding, ordering, strengthening, commanding, receiving, revealing, and anointing, and these correspond, step by step, to the nine orders of angels. In the human mind the first three degrees of the aforementioned orders concern nature; the following three, activity; and the last three, grace. Having obtained these, the soul, entering into itself, enters into the celestial Jerusalem, where, considering the order of the angels, it sees in them God, who dwells in them and performs all their works.[30]

In this interiorization of the notion of hierarchy, Dionysian themes are being used to explore human inwardness, the inwardness of one made in the image and likeness of God.

The other dramatic reinterpretation of a Dionysian theme can likewise be traced back to Thomas Gallus. In this the Dionysian theme of the divine darkness is used to suggest that the soul's way to God is not a way for the mind or intellect at all, but a matter of the soul's loving affection. The most famous representative of this interpretation of Dionysian darkness is the Middle English anonymous treatise of the fourteenth century, *The Cloud of Unknowing*. There Bernard's opposition of knowing and feeling is crossed with the Dionysian imagery of darkness to produce the doctrine that to draw near to God we need to renounce the intellect and reach out into the darkness of ignorance, the 'cloud of unknowing', with a ' sharp dart of longing love'. For Denys the divine darkness lies beyond the farthest effort of the mind, and it is the mind (the *nous*) that enters it: for the author of the *Cloud*, we enter the cloud of unknowing when we renounce the activity of the mind and rely solely on the 'loving power' of the soul. That the author of the *Cloud* has derived this interpretation of Denys from Thomas Gallus is clear from the prologue to his translation of Denys's *Mystical Theology* (or *Hid Divinity*, as he—correctly—translates it), where he acknowledges his debt to the 'Abbot of St Victor' as he mistakenly describes him, and indeed from the translation itself, where the introduction of the phrase 'with affection above mind' into the *Mystical Theology* from Thomas Gallus's commentary transforms Denys's teaching and makes the work of contemplation a matter for the 'loving power' of the soul and not its 'knowing power'.[31]

These two examples suggest that the influence of Denys in the West was very different from his influence in the East. Denys himself represents a kind of synthesis of the theological and philosophical traditions that continued to be influential in Byzantine theology. His influence was easily absorbed and was most deeply felt where he underlined themes already dear to the East: for example, with his lapidary statement of the conviction of God's utter ineffability (the notion of apophatic theology was gratefully taken up in the Byzantine tradition), or in his appreciation of the liturgical worship of the Byzantine Church, sensitive to its dramatic movement and rich symbolism. That the heart of Denys's theology was the praise of God continued to be understood in the East. In the West, the influence of Denys was different mainly because by the time his influence was at all deeply felt—in the twelfth century—Western theology had begun to develop its own characteristic emphases (though many of them can be traced back to St Augustine: the appreciation of inwardness, for example) and the Dionysian corpus is pillaged for themes and imagery which are then used in an entirely different context, and often with a meaning quite foreign to anything Denys might have intended. The influence of Denys in the West is thus much more complex, as Denys is being read in the light of presuppositions that are increasingly remote from him: very much more complex than we have been able to indicate in such a brief sketch. St Thomas Aquinas read Denys with great care and attention: and whole areas of his theology—the doctrine of the divine attributes, angelology, to name but two—are deeply in debt to him. Eckhart, too, read Denys and often quotes him in his sermons: some of his most characteristic themes—for example, his notion of imageless unknowing by which we come close to God—are transpositions of Dionysian themes. In some way, too, Denys influenced the concept of the Dark Night of the Soul, central to the spirituality of St John of the Cross.

One in the West who did respond to the heart of Denys's vision, his understanding of the whole hierarchically ordered cosmos as a hymn in praise of the creator, was Dante, in his great poem, the *Divine Comedy*. Denys is introduced as the one who understood the nature of the angelic hierarchies and Dante represents Gregory the Great, whose influential ordering of the angelic ranks differed (as we have seen) from that of Denys, as opening his eyes in heaven to realize his mistake:

And Dionysius set himself with such zeal
to contemplate these orders
that he named and distributed them as I do;
but later Gregory differed from him,
so that as soon as he opened his eyes in this heaven
he smiled at himself.[32]

But the influence of Denys on Dante goes much further than the matter of the correct order of the angelic ranks: the whole notion of the heaven as light irradiating in splendid multiformity, expressing the outward flow of God's love and the loving response of the cosmos—all this is close to the Dionysian vision, even though other traditions of thought flow into it too.

The primal light that irradiates them all
is received by them in as many ways
as are the splendours with which it is joined,

and therefore, since the affections follow the act of conceiving,
love's sweetness glows variously
in them, more and less.
See now the height and breadth
of the Eternal Goodness, since it has made for itself
so many mirrors in which it is broken,
remaining in itself one as before.[33]

Notes

1   For the influence of Denys on later Christian thought see the series of
     articles in *Dictionnaire de Spiritualité* III (Paris, 1957), cols 286–429
     (some of which have, however, been superseded by more recent
     research).

2   *The Paradise or Garden of the Holy Fathers*, trans. E. A. Wallis
     Budge, 2 vols (London, 1907).

3   For the history of the *Kephalaia Gnostica*, and their influence, see A.
     Guillaumont, *Les "Kephalaia Gnostica" d'Évagre le Pontique* (Paris,
     1962). For a brief account of what was available in Syriac, see Sebastian
     Brock in *The Study of Spirituality*, ed. Cheslyn Jones, Geoffrey Wain-
     wright, Edward Yarnold (London, 1986), pp. 207–9.

4   Surviving works, with Eng. trans. in A. Mingana, *Early Christian
     Mystics*, *Woodbrooke Studies* VII (Cambridge, 1934).

5   Ibid., p. 15.

6   Ibid., p. 11.

7   Ibid., p. 57.

8   Guillaumont, op. cit., pp. 302–32.

9   See Hans Urs von Balthasar, 'Das Scholienwerk des Johannes von
     Scythopolis', *Scholastik* 16 (1940), pp. 16–38; repr., with minor revi-
     sions, in *Kosmische Liturgie* (2nd ed., 1961), pp. 644–72.

10   See H. D. Saffrey, 'Nouveaux liens objectifs entre le Ps-Denys et
     Proclus', *Revue des sciences philosophiques et théologiques* 63 (1979),
     pp. 3–16.

11   E.g. by A. Riou, *Le Monde et l'Église selon Maxime le Confesseur*
     (Paris, 1973), p. 160.

12   St Germanus of Constantinople, *On the Divine Liturgy*, with intro-
     duction, translation and commentary by Paul Meyendorff (Crest-
     wood, NY, 1984), p. 56.

13   See R. Bornert, *Les commentaires byzantins de la divine liturgie du
     VIIe au XVe siècle* (Paris, 1966).

14   E.g., *Theological, Gnostic and Practical Chapters*, II.18 (ed. J. Darrouzès, *Sources Chrétiennes* 51, Paris, 1957, p. 76).

15   *Nicétas Stéthatos, Opuscules et Lettres*, ed. and trans. J. Darrouzès (*Sources Chrétiennes* 81; Paris, 1961).

16   *Centuries* III.42–4.

17   See, e.g., D. Obolensky, *The Byzantine Commonwealth* (London, 1971), pp. 298–300, where Obolensky speaks of events contemporary with Nicetas.

18   See Bishop Kallistos Ware in *The Study of Spirituality* (above, note 3), p. 249.

19   Edited with French trans. by S. Salaville and others (*Sources Chrétiennes* 4 bis; Paris, 1967); Eng. trans. by J. M. Hussey and P. A. McNulty (London, 1966).

20   Eng. trans. by C. J. deCatanzaro (Crestwood, NY, 1974).

21   Especially by Jean Meyendorff: see his *Le Christ dans la pensée byzantine* (Paris, 1969), ch. 5, pp. 121–47, and his 'Notes sur l'influence dionysienne en Orient', *Studia Patristica* 2 (1957), pp. 547–52. Such an attitude is not shared by all modern Orthodox: the late Vladimir Lossky was a notable advocate of Denys.

22   For the Latin story in general see Dom David Knowles, 'The influence of Pseudo-Dionysius on Western mysticism' in *Christian Spirituality. Essays in honour of Gordon Rupp*, ed. Peter Brooks (London, 1975), pp. 79–94.

23   See *Abbot Suger on the Abbey Church of St-Denis and its Art Treasures*, ed., trans. and annotated by E. Panofsky (2nd ed., Princeton, NJ, 1979).

24   See H. Dondaine, *Le Corpus dionysien de l'université de Paris au XIIIe siècle* (Paris, 1953).

25   See E. Boissard, 'S. Bernard et la pseudo-Aréopagite', *Recherches de théologie ancienne et médiévale* 26 (1959), pp. 214–63, which convincingly challenges the conclusions drawn in the article in the *Dictionnaire de Spiritualité* (see note 1 above).

26   See my 'St Bernard and affective mysticism' in *The Influence of St Bernard*, ed. Benedicta Ward SLG (Fairacres Publications, 60; Fairacres, Oxford, 1976), pp. 1–10.

27   See Colin Morris, *The Discovery of the Individual. 1050–1200* (London, 1972).

28   See J. G. Bougerol, 'S. Bonaventure et la hiérarchie dionysienne', *Archives d'histoire doctrinale et littéraire du moyen-âge* 36 (1969), pp. 131–67.

29   See J. Walsh, 'Thomas Gallus et l'effort contemplatif', *Revue d'histoire de la spiritualité* 51 (1975), pp. 17–42.

30 *Itinerarium mentis in Deum* IV.4: in *Works of St Bonaventure*, vol. 2, with trans. by P. Boehner (St Bonaventure, NY, 1956), pp. 75–7.

31 See Dom Justin McCann's note in his edition of *The Cloud of Unknowing* (London, 1924), p. 252.

32 *Paradiso* XXVIII.130–135 (J. D. Sinclair's translation: London, 1958).

33 *Paradiso* XXIX.136–145. For a good discussion of Denys's influence on Dante see E. G. Gardner, *Dante and the Mystics* (London, 1913), pp. 77–110.

8

Conclusion

In a fine essay on the thought of Denys the Areopagite, Bishop Westcott wrote:

> This harmonization of Christianity and Platonism was not
> effected without a sacrifice. It is impossible not to feel in
> Dionysius, in spite of his generous and apostolic aspirations,
> the lack of something which is required for the completeness of
> his own views. He fails indeed by neglecting to take in the
> whole breadth of the Gospel. The central source of his dog-
> matic errors lies where at first it might be least looked for. The
> whole view of life which he offers is essentially individual and
> personal and subjective; the one man is the supreme object in
> whose progress his interest is engaged. Though he gives a
> magnificent view of the mutual coherence of all the parts of the
> moral and physical worlds, yet he turns with the deepest satis-
> faction to the solitary monk, isolated and self-absorbed, as the
> highest type of Christian energy. Though he dwells upon the
> Divine order of the Sacraments, and traces the spiritual signi-
> ficance of each detail in their celebration, yet he looks upon
> them as occasions for instruction and blessing, suggested by
> appointed forms, and not supplied by a Divine gift. He stops
> short of that profounder faith which sees the unity of the
> worlds in the harmonious and yet independent action of deri-
> vative forces; one indeed in their source, and yet regarded as
> separate in their operation. He is still so far overpowered by
> Platonism that he cannot, in speculation as well as in con-

fession, consistently treat man's bodily powers as belonging to the perfection of his nature. The end of the discipline of life is, in his view, to help the believer to cast aside all things that belong to earth, and not to find in them gifts which may by consecration to God become hereafter the beginning of a nobler activity. And so it is that he is unable to see in their full beauty and strength those instincts and faculties of man, by which he is impelled towards social combination, and the divine institutions by which these instincts and faculties are sanctioned and supported.[1]

Anyone who has come so far in this book with any sympathy will find that judgement of Westcott's surprising. Yet Westcott's judgement is, in essence, that of many who deplore the influence of the Areopagite, especially modern Orthodox writers such as John Meyendorff[2] and Alexander Schmemann.[3] Indeed, they repeat what are, fundamentally, Westcott's strictures without finding room for Westcott's admiration—perhaps because the damage they feel Denys to have done seems very close at hand.

The heart of this charge against Denys is *individualism*. But we have seen that the central concepts in Denys's vision—the notions of hierarchy, mutual independence, the dramatic movement of the liturgy (which demands a community in which to move)—all belie such a judgement. Nevertheless such is the nature of Westcott's charge. We must ask ourselves *why* he and others make such a judgement. It is, essentially, because the whole of Denys's vision—cosmic and ecclesial—seems to them to be a *spectacle*.

It is as if someone were to say that the ballet is individualistic. On one level, such a judgement is absurd: ballet requires utmost co-operation and team-spirit from those who dance—if everyone regarded him- or herself as an independent individual, it would be a disaster. On another level, the ballet is a spectacle put on for a group of individuals to watch and admire, by which they are to be uplifted and entranced. Most do not take part: they watch, and their appreciation is individual. For Westcott, Denys's vision is somewhat balletic: a cosmic and ecclesial ballet which most of us are to watch—a long way from the traditional understanding of Christian worship as the worship of the whole community gathered together to give thanks and to celebrate. When Denys calls the laity the 'contemplative order', Westcott understands him to mean 'those who watch'. The real participants are the clergy (and in a way the monks with their 'ascetic' performance).

131

But we have suggested that Denys does not really regard hierarchy as something imposed on 'us' and independent of 'us': rather it *consists* of us. The theophany that the cosmos is, that the hierarchies are, is not over against us: we are part of it. If Denys's vision *is* balletic, then we are all meant to join in the dance.

Perhaps the problem lies in the word 'hierarchy'. We do not nowadays in the West think naturally in hierarchical terms. We presuppose that all men and women are equal; we tend to see society on some sort of 'social contract' model: we have (or can be regarded as having) agreed together to form a society, by accepting the constraints that living together imposes. Our notion of community tends to mean 'doing things together'. Applied to the liturgy, such an understanding of community produces the notion of worship which is becoming more and more prevalent in the Christian West. Christian worship is everyone doing everything together: we sing hymns, we repeat prayers together; if anything is said, then we all want to be able to hear it, so that we can all 'take part'. It was not always like that (nor is it yet in the Orthodox Church). Some parts of the liturgy used to be silent, other things would be going on at the same time, there was no 'single line' in the liturgy that all should follow. The idea that there should be—at least as far as the part sung by the choir is concerned—is not new. Church authorities have long deplored polyphony and have never appreciated the great, incomprehensible bursts of praise produced in baroque Mass settings by compressed *Glorias* and *Credos*. But this idea of community and communal worship really *is* individualistic: it envisages a collection of individuals doing everything together (as far as possible).

The notion of hierarchy suggests something very different. It suggests a community that is essentially structured, where there are genuinely different roles, and the putting together of those different roles creates something new and different from all the parts that go to make it. Such an understanding of an essentially hierarchical society is not something new in Christian history with Denys; on the contrary, it is very ancient. We can find it at the end of the first century in the first Epistle of Clement of Rome:

> For to the high priest [i.e., the bishop] his proper ministrations are allotted, and to the priests the proper place has been appointed, and on levites [i.e., deacons] their proper services (*diakoniai*) have been imposed. The layman is bound by the ordinances for the laity. Let each of us, brothers, celebrate the

132

> Eucharist to God in his own order, having a good conscience,
> and not transgressing the prescribed rule of his ministry, in
> reverence.[4]

And Clement is only echoing the words of St Paul in one of his own letters to the Corinthians (1 Cor 12:4–30). The idea of a hierarchical society—even though the word *hierarchy* is Denys's—is a more natural presupposition in late antique society than any other: certainly more natural than our own notions of a 'social contract' which only go back to the Enlightenment (and have hardly stood the test of even that short time).

If these considerations can be admitted as having much weight, it would seem that Westcott, in accusing Denys of individualism, is picking out of Denys's system an individualism he finds there because it is the only part of Denys's view of things that reflects his own, fundamentally individualistic, presuppositions. In other words, it is Westcott who is the individualist, not Denys, and Westcott shows this by finding it impossible to understand Denys except in an individualist way. Denys's strong sense of hierarchy excludes Westcott (and most of us) and so Denys's vision appears to him as a spectacle, for the appraisal of the individual—or perhaps as a kind of distorting mirror, in which we see our own features exaggerated.

Such a conclusion is not very surprising when we reflect how very different societies can be and how difficult it is to appreciate a society that seems strange to us. Mary Douglas, in her *Natural Symbols*,[5] has suggested how we might estimate the different ways in which a society can function, and the way these determine the world-view of that society, and so avoid the mistake of measuring all societies against our experience of modern, liberal, essentially individualistic society. Perhaps Mary Douglas herself shows some nostalgia for a more structured society, more capable of supporting a symbolic universe, than ours: it would certainly seem that such a nostalgia, or at least a sympathy for such a society, is necessary for appreciating Denys and his vision of society and the cosmos. His society is certainly one with both strong 'grid' and strong 'group' characteristics, to use Mary Douglas's terms (that is, a society in which there is a powerful system of shared values, and a strong sense that the individual's values are controlled by the pressure of others), though it does not fit too easily into her categories, perhaps because the achievement of Denys was to find room in his vision of society for a variety of types. While his society as a whole is highly structured, he finds place in it for the monk, the solitary, which would seem to be a low-grid type (in other words, his values are largely ones he has discovered for himself). Denys's attitude to the problem of evil—at least as manifest in DN IV—is also that which is characteristic of the low-grid type.

The point of bringing in Mary Douglas's ideas here is not to herald a further reconsideration of the Dionysian vision, using her categories, but rather to strike a warning-note about how easy it is for us to dismiss a way of thinking that is rooted in a society very differently conceived from our own. Such a consideration suggests caution, and caution can be a form of respect. Denys's vision is remarkable because, on the one hand, his understanding of hierarchy makes possible a rich symbolic system in terms of which we can understand God and the cosmos and our place within it, and, on the other, he finds room within this strictly hierarchical society for an escape from it, beyond it, by transcending symbols and realizing directly one's relationship with God as his creature, the creature of his love.

There is space within the Dionysian universe for a multitude of ways of responding to God's love. That spaciousness is worth exploring: and therein, perhaps, lies the enduring value of the vision of Denys the Areopagite.

Notes

1 B. F. Westcott, *Essays in the History of Religious Thought in the West* (London, 1891), pp. 189–91 (the complete essay is found on pp. 142–93).

2 J. Meyendorff, *Le Christ dans la pensée byzantine* (Paris, 1969), p. 147.

3 A. Schmemann, *Introduction to Liturgical Theology* (Eng. trans., London/Portland, ME, 1966), p. 155 (the 'ascetic' is to be understood as 'individualistic': see pp. 106f.)

4 *I Clement* 40f.

5 Mary Douglas, *Natural Symbols* (Pelican ed., Harmondsworth, Middx, 1973).

Made in the USA
Lexington, KY
09 January 2015

3846497R00083